OUR BEST FRIENDS

The Dachshund

OUR BEST FRIENDS

OUR BEST FRIENDS

The Dachshund

Karen Schweitzer

ELDORADO INK

Produced by OTTN Publishing, Stockton, New Jersey

Eldorado Ink
PO Box 100097
Pittsburgh, PA 15233
www.eldoradoink.com

CPSIA compliance information: Batch#101909-3. For further information, contact
Eldorado Ink at info@eldoradoink.com.

First printing

1 3 5 7 9 8 6 4 2

Library of Congress Cataloging-in-Publication Data

Schweitzer, Karen.
   The dachshund / Karen Schweitzer.
      p. cm. — (Our best friends)
   Includes bibliographical references and index.
   ISBN 978-1-932904-59-8
   1. Dachshunds—Juvenile literature. I. Title.
   SF429.D25S38 2010
   636.753'8—dc22

                          2009041440

Photo credits: Dan Bennett (http://www.flickr.com/photos/soggydan/3623681505/in/
set-72157619629070319), 33; Dan Bennett (http://www.flickr.com/photos/soggydan/
3657333885/), 89; Lee Coursey (http://www.flickr.com/photos/leeco/304282455/), 91;
© istockphoto.com/Angelcarver, 96; © istockphoto.com/lesliejmorris, 97; © istockphoto.com/
nano, 94; © istockphoto.com/superchappie, 65; © istockphoto.com/tdargon, front cover (top
inset); © istockphoto.com/YinYang, 87; Used under license from Shutterstock, Inc., 3, 8, 10, 11
(both), 13, 14, 16, 20, 23, 24, 25, 26, 35, 36, 37, 40, 42, 43, 44, 45, 49, 51, 53, 54, 57, 58, 59,
60, 62, 63, 66, 70, 71, 74, 77, 80, 86, 92, 93, 98, 99, front cover (main, middle inset, bottom
inset), back cover.

**For information about custom editions, special sales, or premiums,
please contact our special sales department at info@eldoradoink.com.**

TABLE OF CONTENTS

Introduction

GARY KORSGAARD, DVM

The mutually beneficial relationship between humans and animals began long before the dawn of recorded history. Archaeologists believe that humans began to capture and tame wild goats, sheep, and pigs more than 9,000 years ago. These animals were then bred for specific purposes, such as providing humans with a reliable source of food or providing furs and hides that could be used for clothing or the construction of dwellings.

Other animals had been sought for companionship and assistance even earlier. The dog, believed to be the first animal domesticated, began living and working with Stone Age humans in Europe more than 14,000 years ago. Some archaeologists believe that wild dogs and humans were drawn together because both hunted the same prey. By taming and training dogs, humans became more effective hunters. Dogs, meanwhile, enjoyed the social contact with humans and benefited from greater access to food and warm shelter. Dogs soon became beloved pets as well as trusted workers. This can be seen from the many artifacts depicting dogs that have been found at ancient sites in Asia, Europe, North America, and the Middle East.

The earliest domestic cats appeared in the Middle East about 5,000 years ago. Small wild cats were probably first attracted to human settlements because plenty of rodents could be found wherever harvested grain was stored. Cats played a useful role in hunting and killing these pests, and it is likely that grateful humans rewarded them for this assistance. Over time, these small cats gave up some of their aggressive wild behaviors and began living among humans. Cats eventually became so popular in ancient Egypt that they were believed to possess magical powers. Cat statues were placed outside homes to ward off evil spirits, and mummified cats were included in royal tombs to accompany their owners into the afterlife.

Today, few people believe that cats have supernatural powers, but most pet owners feel a magical bond with their pets, whether they are dogs, cats, hamsters, rabbits, horses, or parrots. The lives of pets and their people become inextricably intertwined, providing strong emotional and physical rewards for both humans and animals. People of all ages can benefit from the loving companionship of a pet. Not surprisingly, then, pet ownership is widespread. Recent statistics indicate that about 60 percent of all households in the United States and Canada have at least one pet, while the figure is close to 50 percent of households in the United Kingdom. For millions of people, therefore, pets truly have become their "best friends."

Finding the best animal friend can be a challenge, however. Not only are there many types of domesticated pets, but each has specific needs, characteristics, and personality traits. Even within a category of pets, such as dogs, different breeds will flourish in different surroundings and with different treatment. For example, a German Shepherd may not be the right pet for a person living in a cramped urban apartment; that person might be better off caring for a smaller dog like a Toy Poodle or Shih Tzu, or perhaps a cat. On the other hand, an active person who loves the outdoors may prefer the companion-ship of a Labrador Retriever to that of a small dog or a passive indoor pet like a goldfish or hamster.

The joys of pet ownership come with certain responsibilities. Bringing a pet into your home and your neighborhood obligates you to care for and train the pet properly. For example, a dog must be housebroken, taught to obey your commands, and trained to behave appropriately when he encounters other people or animals. Owners must also be mindful of their pet's particular nutritional and medical needs.

The purpose of the OUR BEST FRIENDS series is to provide a helpful and comprehensive introduction to pet ownership. Each book contains the basic information a prospective pet owner needs in order to choose the right pet for his or her situation and to care for that pet throughout the pet's lifetime. Training, socialization, proper nutrition, potential medical issues, and the legal responsibilities of pet ownership are thoroughly explained and discussed, and an abundance of expert tips and suggestions are offered. Whether it is a hamster, corn snake, guinea pig, or Labrador Retriever, the books in the OUR BEST FRIENDS series provide everything the reader needs to know about how to have a happy, well-adjusted, and well-behaved pet.

Dachshunds are smart, lively dogs. They are admired as much for their friendly personalities as for their long, low bodies. These lovable, playful dogs make great companions for children.

CHAPTER ONE

Is a Dachshund Right for You?

The distinctive shape of the Dachshund makes this dog one of the most recognizable breeds in the world. Dachshund bodies are long and low to the ground, while their legs are very short. These characteristics have earned the breed many nicknames, such as "wiener dogs" and "sausage dogs."

Dachshunds make great companions because of their affectionate natures and happy-go-lucky attitudes. Dachshunds are also known for their cleverness, playfulness, and determination. These endearing attributes, among others, have made the Dachshund a favorite dog breed in the United States, Great Britain, and Germany. According to

American Kennel Club (AKC) dog registration statistics, for the past several decades Dachshunds have consistently ranked among the top 10 most popular breeds in the United States. They are particularly popular in urban areas where space is limited and smaller dogs are more common.

It is important to note, however, that this breed isn't for everyone. Dachshunds are very social creatures, and will be happiest when they have someone nearby to interact with on a regular basis. If left alone for too long, Dachshunds can be mischievous and destructive. Dachshunds are also very vocal. They frequently bark when they are stressed or excited, and often make noise to defend their territory and their family from approaching visitors.

PHYSICAL CHARACTERISTICS

What initially attracts most people to a Dachshund is the breed's unique appearance. These dogs have long bodies, short legs, prominent chests, alert expressions, and dark soulful eyes. They are bred in two sizes: standard and miniature. Standard Dachshunds weigh between 16 and 32 pounds (7 and 14 kg). Miniature Dachshunds are significantly smaller, weighing less than 11 pounds (5 kg). Purebred Dachshunds can have one of three different types of coats: smooth, wirehaired, and longhaired.

SMOOTH: Smooth Dachshunds (such as the one pictured below) are probably the most recognizable version of the breed. These dogs have short hair that is shiny and silky to the touch. They are

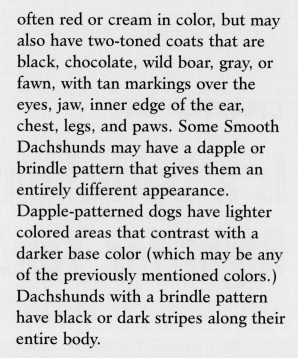

often red or cream in color, but may also have two-toned coats that are black, chocolate, wild boar, gray, or fawn, with tan markings over the eyes, jaw, inner edge of the ear, chest, legs, and paws. Some Smooth Dachshunds may have a dapple or brindle pattern that gives them an entirely different appearance. Dapple-patterned dogs have lighter colored areas that contrast with a darker base color (which may be any of the previously mentioned colors.) Dachshunds with a brindle pattern have black or dark stripes along their entire body.

WIREHAIRED: Wirehaired Dachshunds (like the one pictured at the top of the opposite page) have a very different type of coat than the Smooth Dachshund. As the name implies, Wirehaired Dachshunds have a short, wiry outer coat. The hair is close to the body and rough to the touch. Underneath and between the coarse hairs is a fine, soft undercoat.

From a distance, the Wirehaired Dachshund looks a lot like the Smooth Dachshund. The only noticeable difference is in

This Smooth Dachshund is black with tan markings—one of the most common coat appearances among members of the breed.

the face. Wirehaired Dachshunds have a distinctive beard and furry eyebrows. Most have coats that are various shades of red, wild boar, tan, or black. However, any coloring or markings that can be found on a Smooth Dachshund can also be seen on a Wirehaired Dachshund.

LONGHAIRED: Longhaired Dachshunds (such as the one pictured below) are built just like Smooth Dachshunds and Wirehaired Dachshunds, but their hair is longer, particularly under the neck and body, on the ears, and behind the legs.

This black-and-tan Wirehaired Dachshund's body is covered with a thick coat of short, coarse hairs. Beneath lies a softer undercoat of short hairs.

The hair of a Longhaired Dachshund is very silky and may sometimes appear wavy. Coat coloring and markings are similar to those of a Smooth Dachshund.

A DACHSHUND'S ROLE IN YOUR LIFE

Although Dachshunds are relatively small, dogs of this breed do not lack personality. They are independent

To look his best, a Longhaired Dachshund will require considerably more grooming time than a Smooth Dachshund. Red is the most common coat color found in all three varieties of the Dachshund breed.

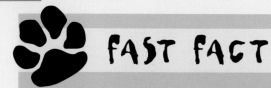

FAST FACT

The name "Dachshund" (pronounced DAHKS-hoont) comes from the German words *dachs* and *hund*, which mean "badger dog." These dogs were originally bred to chase badgers into their underground tunnels, so that the dog's owner could dig up and kill the badger.

and courageous, and are generally willing to challenge a larger person or animal. Their spirit and boldness sometimes makes Dachshunds difficult to train, but owners who are patient and determined can almost always modify bad behavior. Dachshunds love people and will do their best to make their owners happy once a bond has been established. This willingness to please is one of the many things that make Dachshunds good companion dogs.

Of course, there are many other roles that a Dachshund can play in a dog owner's life. This breed is a popular entrant in tracking, agility, earthdog, and field competitions. Dachshunds can also participate in conformation shows, at which the entrants are judged on how well their physical characteristics match the standard for this breed. Training Dachshunds for these events will

take time, but for some people the payoff is worth the effort.

Dachshunds can even be useful companions for hunters. These dogs were originally bred for this purpose, and in Europe today Dachshunds are commonly used to hunt small game, such as rabbits, foxes, and woodchucks. These dogs can also be used to flush birds and track wounded deer.

THE BEST ENVIRONMENT FOR A DACHSHUND

Although Dachshunds are very adaptable dogs, not every environment is suitable for this breed. Dachshunds need to be with people who can give them attention. A Dachshund that is left alone for too long will find ways to make trouble.

It is also important for dogs of this breed to have a warm, dry place

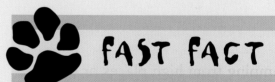

FAST FACT

The Dachshund is a member of a breed group known as a scenthound. This name designates hunting dogs that track game animals using their sensitive noses to follow the scent. Other German scenthound breeds include the Hanoverian Hound, the Bavarian Mountain Hound, the Westphalian Dachsbracke, and the Deutsche Bracke.

Miniature Dachshunds resemble their larger breed counterparts in all respects except size. A Miniature Dachshund should be under six inches (15 cm) high and weigh less than 11 pounds (5 kg).

to live and sleep. Dachshunds enjoy the outdoors but they are not "outside dogs." A Dachshund would much rather lounge at the feet, or on the lap, of his owner in front of a fire than shiver in a cold, damp outdoor kennel.

Dachshunds enjoy plenty of activities, including walks and games of fetch. However, Dachshund owners should make sure their pets avoid jumping from high places or other high-impact activities. Because of their unique build, Dachshunds that are subjected to excessive jumping, or even too much stair climbing, often end up with serious and debilitating vertebrae conditions.

In short, the best environment for a Dachshund is one that provides a lot of love and appreciation, a decent amount of fun and mental stimulation, and just enough pampering to make a dog comfortable.

BASIC COSTS ASSOCIATED WITH DACHSHUND OWNERSHIP

Owning a dog can be expensive. In addition to the purchase price, there are veterinary costs and various day-to-day expenses. It is not unusual for a Dachshund owner to spend hundreds, and possibly thousands, of dollars each year to care for her pet. Before purchasing a Dachshund, prospective owners should understand the basic costs associated with responsible dog ownership, including the following:

ROUTINE VETERINARY CARE: Every Dachshund needs an initial veterinary exam as well as annual wellness exams. Healthy senior dogs (age nine and above) should be examined every six months. The cost of veterinary care can vary, depending on the vet and the thoroughness of the exam. On average, Dachshund owners can expect to pay anywhere from $20 to $200 for each examination.

PARASITE TESTS AND PREVENTION: Internal parasites, such as heartworms, roundworms, and tapeworms, can make a Dachshund very ill and may even cause death in extreme cases. Dachshund puppies need to be tested for parasites at their first veterinary exam, and once a year thereafter. If worms are present, the veterinarian will provide medication to kill the parasites. If not, the vet will supply preventive medication to discourage infestation.

Typically, the costs of lab testing and medication range between $100 and $150 each year for healthy dogs.

IMMUNIZATIONS: Every Dachshund puppy requires a series of inoculations to protect against diseases like distemper, hepatitis, leptospirosis, parainfluenza, and parvovirus. At about six months old, puppies need a rabies shot. After receiving initial inoculations, adult dogs need regular booster shots to protect against these diseases. Other immunizations a Dachshund may receive include vaccinations against coronavirus, kennel cough, and Lyme disease. The cost for immunizations varies, but owners can expect to spend up to $150 per year.

SPAYING OR NEUTERING: Dachshunds that will not be bred or

Dachshunds need safe chew toys to keep them entertained while their owners are away. Dogs that do not have a distraction will frequently chew on things they aren't supposed to have.

entered into formal competitions should be spayed or neutered when they are about six months old. This will prevent unwanted pregnancies and may reduce the likelihood of infections or life-threatening illnesses, such as certain cancers. Spaying or neutering is a onetime cost that usually ranges from $50 to $300.

GROOMING SUPPLIES: Compared to some breeds, Dachshunds are relatively easy to groom. However, these dogs will need to be brushed at least once a week and bathed on a regular basis. Longhaired Dachshunds require more brushing and bathing than other Dachshunds.

Dog owners can clean and brush their pets at home, or take them to a professional groomer. Home care is a less-costly option, although there will be an expense for brushes, dog shampoo, a shower nozzle, nail clippers, and other necessary equipment. Professional groomers usually charge between $30 and $150 per session, so the annual cost of grooming can mount rapidly.

FLEA AND TICK PREVENTION: External parasites like fleas and ticks live off the blood of their hosts. Flea bites cause severe itching and discomfort, and a severe flea infestation can result in hair loss, skin infections, anemia, and allergic reactions. Ticks can cause similar problems, and certain kinds of ticks carry Lyme disease as well. A Dachshund owner can expect to spend between $50 and $100 on flea and tick prevention each year. Treatment for a flea infestation is considerably higher than preventive care.

FOOD: Dachshunds love food and will usually eat as much as they can. An adult Dachshund will need between half a cup and two cups of high-quality dry dog food each day, depending on his size and activity level. The cost of food varies greatly, depending on the brand and the ingredients: the higher the quality, the higher the price. Dachshund owners can expect to spend $500 or more each year on food alone.

MISCELLANEOUS COSTS: Caring for a Dachshund requires other supplies as well. These include, but are not limited to: a crate, bedding, a collar, a leash, dog bowls, toys, treats, dog tags, and training supplies. There is really no limit to what you can buy or how much you can spend on your canine companion.

CHAPTER TWO

Dachshund History and Breed Standard

The modern Dachshund breed originated in Germany during the 1400s. German hounds called Deutsche Bracken were cross-bred with terrier-type dogs to develop a small but energetic scenthound useful for tracking badgers, rabbits, foxes, and other small game into their underground burrows. The Dachshund's long, pointed nose, elongated body, loud bark, and courageous personality made them perfect for this task. These hounds were sometimes referred to as Teckel—a German nickname for dogs with scent-tracking capabilities. By the 1600s, the name *Dachshund* was used to refer to a specific breed of shorthaired hunting dogs. It wasn't long before Dachshunds had

Dachshunds were originally bred to hunt small game, such as badgers and rabbits.

spread beyond Germany and become popular in other European countries.

The first German studbook for Dachshunds was published in 1879. This book included a registry of Dachshunds considered to be pure-breds, as well as a detailed list of the breed's most desirable characteristics. In 1888 the first Dachshund club was formed in Germany. Known as the Berlin Teckelklub, this organization published its own studbook in 1890 and worked hard to promote interest in the breed.

Dachshunds were still used primarily for hunting during the late nineteenth century. However, around this time a number of Dachshund breeders began producing and raising dogs for the show ring. Clubs were soon formed for aficionados of different types of Dachshunds. There was a German Hunting Dachshund Club, a German Working Dachshund Club, and a Miniature Dachshund Club.

There were even clubs devoted to the different Dachshund coat types. The original Dachshunds had smooth, short coats. Over time, breeders developed a longer-haired version of the dog, possibly by cross-breeding Smooth Dachshunds with the German Spaniel, another type of hunting dog. The Wirehaired Dachshund appeared in the late 1800s. This dog may have been the result of crossing Smooth Dachshunds with Schnauzers or German Wirehaired Pointers.

THE DACHSHUND IN AMERICA

Dachshunds began appearing in the United States during the late nineteenth century. Some arrived with immigrants, while others were imported by wealthy dog-lovers who wanted show-quality dogs. In 1895 the Dachshund Club of America was established to promote the breed. Although the club did hold hunting trials, for the most part Dachshunds were bred as pets and show dogs in the United States.

By 1913, Dachshunds were among the 10 favorite dog breeds in the United States, according to AKC statistics. Artists and illustrators often featured the dogs in their works because of the Dachshund's unusual shape and attractive facial

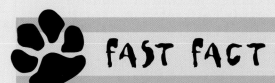

FAST FACT

It was the English who originally turned the Dachshund from hunting dogs into pets. The breed was a favorite among nineteenth century British aristocrats, including Queen Victoria. The first Dachshund Club was formed in England in 1881.

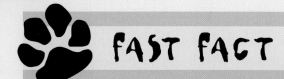

expressions. However, the breed's association with Germany caused the dogs to fall out of favor during the First World War (1914–1918). In America, there was a backlash against German culture when the United States declared war against Germany and its allies in April 1917. As a result, Dachshund breeding nearly ended in the United States until after the war.

The lovable Dachshund eventually won back the hearts of Americans. By 1940, Dachshunds were again ranked among the 10 most popular AKC breeds. According to the most recent AKC statistics, Dachshunds are ranked seventh in popularity among American dog breeds.

BREED STANDARDS AND CONFORMATION

For each breed of purebred dog, there is a parent club that is organized and led by experienced breeders and other fanciers of that breed. Each parent club develops a written description of the perfect dog of that breed, and this is the criterion by which dogs of that breed are judged in the show ring. This description is known as the Standard of Perfection, or the breed standard. The Standard of Perfection always describes the proper appearance and gait, and many standards also discuss the ideal temperament and personality characteristics of the breed. Reputable breeders strive to produce dogs that conform to the Standard of Perfection as closely as possible.

In the breed standard adopted by the American Kennel Club, the Dachshund is described as a "lively breed" with a "keen sense of smell" and a "friendly personality." The AKC breed standard is essentially the same for both Standard Dachshunds and Miniature Dachshunds. The only differences have to do with weight and size.

SIZE: Miniature Dachshunds weigh 11 pounds (5 kg) or less. Standard Dachshunds weigh between 16 and 32 pounds (7 and 14 kg). Both types of Dachshunds should have long bodies and short legs that place them low to the ground.

STRUCTURE: All Dachshunds should be well-balanced and carry their heads confidently. When viewed in profile, a Dachshund's neck should slope gracefully into his shoulders. The back must be straight between the withers (shoulders) and a slightly arched loin.

CHEST: The chest should be strong with a prominent breastbone. The bone should be so prominent that a

COMMON DACHSHUND FAULTS

Just about every Dachshund deviates from the AKC breed standard in some small way. Deviations are known as faults. Dachshunds that have too many faults may be barred from participating in certain AKC-sanctioned competitions. Faults common to the Dachshund breed include:

- Awkward or cramped movement
- Skull that is too broad or too narrow
- Dull eyes
- Wall eyes (this is allowed in Dachshunds with dappled coats)
- An even bite
- Pointed, narrow, or folded ears
- Arched back
- Excessive wrinkling on the skin
- White on the chest (this is acceptable, but not desirable)
- Hair that is too long or thick (Smooth Dachshund)
- Long, curly, or wavy hair (Wirehaired Dachshund)
- Soft hair in the outercoat or a missing undercoat (Wirehaired Dachshund)
- Curly or equally long hair over the whole body (Longhaired Dachshund)
- Leathery ears (Smooth Dachshund)
- Brush tail (Smooth Dachshund)
- Hairless tail (Smooth Dachshund)
- Flag tail (Wirehaired Dachshund)
- Curved tail
- Twisted or kinked tail
- Legs that turn in or out
- Rolling or high-stepping gait
- Shyness
- Knuckling over of the front legs (automatic disqualification)

Because the Dachshund is a hunting dog, hunting wounds and scars are not considered faults. Instead, they are viewed as symbols of honor and bravery.

depression or dimple is evident on either side. When viewed from the front, both the thorax and the enclosing structure of the ribs should appear oval. When viewed in profile, the front leg should hide the lowest point of a Dachshund's breast.

FOREQUARTERS AND HINDQUARTERS: A Dachshund's forelegs and thighs should be strong and cleanly muscled. Ideally, the upper leg will be the same length as the shoulder blade. The foreleg must be short, pliable, and curved slightly inward so that the front does not appear perfectly straight. Together, the shoulder blades and forelegs create a parenthesis or wraparound effect around the ribcage. In the hindquarters, the pelvis, thighs, and rear pasterns should be the same length. The rear pasterns must be upright and parallel when viewed from behind.

FEET: All four feet must have compact, well-arched toes. The pads on the bottom of the feet should be tough and thick. The hind paws are typically smaller than the front paws. Rear dewclaws should be removed, and front dewclaws may be removed.

The American Kennel Club posts the official breed standard developed by the Dachshund Club of America on its Web site at http://www.akc.org/breeds/dachshund/index.cfm.

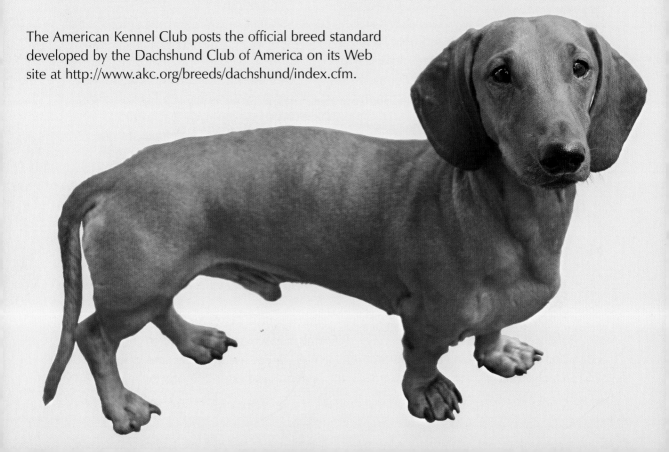

MUZZLE: The muzzle of a Dachshund should be finely formed and almost Roman in appearance. It is important that the head taper uniformly to the tip of the nose. The jaw should also be well formed, with strong teeth that fit closely together in a scissor bite.

EYES: A Dachshund's eyes should be almond-shaped, medium in size, very dark in color, and set beneath prominent bridge bones. This breed's eyes should be expressive and alert.

EARS: Ears should be rounded and moderate in length. Both ears should begin near the top of the head but not too far forward.

TAIL: The tail should extend cleanly as though it is an extension of the spine. It should not be carried too gaily, nor should it be kinked, twisted, or curved in any way.

GAIT: Freedom of movement is very important for all Dachshunds. Movement must be fluid and smooth and should never appear choppy. Although the legs do not move in parallel planes, the feet should travel parallel with the line of motion versus swinging out or crossing over. Rear pads that are fully exposed during rear extension equal correct movement.

TEMPERAMENT: Dachshunds are expected to be clever, lively, and courageous. Shyness is a serious fault in a show dog.

SPECIAL COAT CHARACTERISTICS

SMOOTH DACHSHUND: The Smooth Dachshund should have a short, smooth coat, soft ears, and a tail that tapers gradually to a point. The coat can be one-colored, two-colored, dappled, sable-patterned, or brindle-patterned. One-colored Dachshunds are usually red and cream, but may also have dark-colored hairs throughout their body. Their noses and nails should be black. Two-colored Dachshunds may be black, chocolate, wild boar (black with an undercoat of light brown hairs, which can be seen around the eyes, nose, and underside of the body), gray (called "blue") or fawn (called "Isabella"). Each color is complimented with either tan or cream-colored markings over the eyes, jaw, inner edge

FAST FACT

The term "double dapple" is sometimes used to describe Dachshund coats that have white coloring mixed with the dapple pattern.

of the ear, chest, legs, and paws. Two-colored Dachshunds should have a dark brown nose and nails, though self-colored is also acceptable. Black Dachshunds are an exception; their nose and nails should be black in color. Dappled Dachshunds should have a consistent pattern of light-colored areas over a darker base color. Nose and nail color is similar to that of two-colored Dachshunds. Dark eyes and blue (wall) eyes are common among Dappled Dachshunds. Both are equally acceptable. Brindle-patterned Dachshunds are tan with black or dark stripes over their entire body. Dachshunds with a sable pattern are red with an overlay of dark, uniform hairs. Their eyes, nose, and nails should be black.

WIREHAIRED DACHSHUND: Wirehaired Dachshunds have an outer coat that is tight, short, thick, rough, and hard to the touch. They also have an undercoat with softer, shorter hairs. The hair on the ears is very soft and feels smooth to the

THE AMERICAN KENNEL CLUB

The American Kennel Club (AKC) is a nonprofit organization that maintains a purebred dog registry. The group, founded in 1884, tracks data and statistics for 157 dog breeds. The AKC records puppy births, registrations for individual dogs, and titles earned in dog shows and other events.

For a Dachshund to be registered with the AKC, the dog's breeder or owner must prove that his parents were previously registered with the AKC. If this is not possible, the AKC will conduct special research to determine whether the dog is eligible to be included in its registry of purebred dogs.

In addition to maintaining its registry, the AKC sponsors a variety of events that are held by member clubs, such as the Dachshund Club of America. These events include dog shows, agility trials, tracking tests, and obedience competitions. The AKC sanctions and promotes events to uphold the breed standard and attract interest from spectators.

Other AKC objectives include advancing the study of purebred dogs and promoting the health and well-being of all dogs. The AKC prides itself on being an advocate for dog owners. You can learn more about the AKC by visiting the club online at www.akc.org.

Purebred Dachshunds come in a variety of acceptable coat colors.

touch. The Wirehaired Dachshund has a very distinctive face compared to other Dachshunds. A beard is clearly present, as are eyebrows. The tail is also different in that it has thick hairs. All colors that are considered acceptable for a Smooth Dachshund are also acceptable for a Wirehaired Dachshund. Wild boar, red, black, and tan are the most common colors.

LONGHAIRED DACHSHUND:

Longhaired Dachshunds have a sleek, glistening coat. Hair is often wavy and is always longer on the forechest, under the neck and body, on the ears, and behind the legs. Long hair is also present on the tail and should form a flag. All colors that are considered acceptable for a Smooth Dachshund are also acceptable for a Longhaired Dachshund.

CHAPTER THREE

Choosing the Right Dachshund

Once you've decided that a Dachshund is the right breed for you, the next step is to find the right dog. While all Dachshunds share certain physical characteristics, no two individual dogs are exactly alike. Some of them will be the kind of dog you're looking for, while others will have traits that don't appeal to you.

Choosing the right Dachshund will be easier if you have some idea about what you would like your dog to accomplish. If you want a show dog, it is essential that you find a Dachshund that matches the breed standard as closely as possible. If, on the other hand, you're just looking for a companion or lap dog, your

When evaluating a litter of Dachshund puppies, watch how each puppy reacts to the other dogs and people in the room.

own personal standards are more important. Keep in mind that a dog that has been well bred is less likely to suffer from genetic defects and other problems that can affect his health later in life.

FACTORS TO CONSIDER

GENDER: One thing a prospective Dachshund owner must decide is whether to acquire a male or female dog. The differences between male and female Dachshunds are minor. This is especially true of dogs that have been spayed or neutered. Male dogs are more likely to mark their territory with urine than female dogs. Intact males are also driven to roam—they'll try to escape from your yard to find a female in heat—and are more likely to react aggressively toward other dogs. Intact females will experience a regular heat cycle, which is typically accompanied by light bleeding or discharge that can stain carpets or furniture. Neutering or spaying reduces or eliminates these problems.

AGE: Potential dog owners can decide whether they are interested in acquiring a puppy or an adult dog. Each option has advantages and disadvantages. It is fun to watch puppies grow, but they require a lot of time and attention. They are a good choice for patient people with time to properly train and socialize a dog.

An older dog may already be housetrained and know some obedience cues and other useful skills. You'll also have a better idea about his temperament before you bring him home than you would with a puppy. However, if you're adopting an adult dog from a shelter or rescue organization, he may exhibit bad behaviors, such as aggression or fear.

Before bringing a Dachshund into your home, consider whether certain traits or characteristics will be more appropriate for your family and lifestyle.

These behaviors might be the reason his original owner abandoned the dog. In the right home and under the right care, nearly any adult dog will be able to overcome emotional and physical challenges, but they are not for everyone.

ABILITIES: Those who want to show a Dachshund competitively must find a dog that conforms to the breed standard. If a show dog has too many faults, he will not do well in competition. Show dogs must also have the right temperament for the ring. It will be difficult, if not impossible, to turn a shy or stubborn Dachshund into a champion.

Good training and the right kind of stimulation can strengthen and enhance any dog's inherited potential, but for your Dachshund to excel at a particular competitive sport or activity, the potential must be present in the first place. You're more likely to find that potential in a pup whose parents and other relatives already

demonstrate ability in the sport or activity of your choice.

Owners who are looking for a pet or companion can be more flexible. A flawed bite, curved tail, or wrinkly skin are of little consequence when it comes to a dog who will be sharing a couch or a lively game of fetch with his owner. What's most important is that the chosen companion's personality is compatible with that of his new family.

WHERE TO FIND THE RIGHT DACHSHUND

Compared to some breeds, Dachshunds are not hard to find. Their position as one of the most popular dog breeds in the United States ensures that Dachshunds can almost always be found wherever dogs are sold. Of course, not every Dachshund seller is a good choice.

Generally, the best place to

The breeder may choose a puppy that she thinks will be right for you.

There usually is very little difference between the price a novice breeder will charge for a Dachshund and the price an established breeder will charge.

purchase a purebred Dachshund puppy is from a responsible and experienced breeder who is dedicated to raising healthy Dachshunds with appropriate temperaments. Such a breeder will make sure that each puppy's parents are free from hereditary health problems. Good breeders socialize their puppies before placing them in a new home, which helps to ensure good behavior later in the dog's life. Reputable breeders are also prepared to answer questions before the sale of a puppy, and will be there to help with problems after the purchase.

Although Dachshunds can be found in pet stores, do some research before buying. Some pet stores have good reputations for offering healthy animals for sale. Other stores put profit ahead of their dogs' health. These stores sell dogs from puppy mills—kennels that breed large numbers of dogs under terrible conditions. In these settings, dogs are very rarely bred responsibly,

and they are almost never given adequate love or medical attention. Females are usually bred every heat cycle until they can no longer carry puppies to term. Very few of the puppies that come from these mills have been socialized properly. As a result, the puppies often have behavioral problems that make them difficult to train, and they may have health problems as well.

Older puppies and adult dogs can be found through animal shelters or rescue operations. Approximately one-third of all shelter and rescue dogs are purebreds, which means that the chance of finding a purebred Dachshund from these sources is relatively high. At the same time, a shelter or rescue dog generally costs much less than a dog bought from a breeder.

Adoption can be a very rewarding experience, but it does come with challenges. Many dogs are in shelters

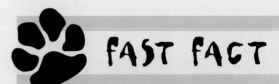

Receiving registration papers doesn't guarantee that a puppy will be healthy and well bred. However, if a breeder will not be able to provide registration papers for his puppies, you should consider buying from another breeder.

because of a change in their owner's situation—for example, the owner had to move to a new apartment which doesn't allow pets. But some are there because of abuse, or because of bad behavior that the previous owner couldn't handle. There is a chance that behavioral issues will surface once you take your new pet home. Such problems can be trying, but they are not impossible to resolve. Dachshunds are intelligent and adaptable, so an adult Dachshund brought into a loving home will almost certainly thrive if the humans around him are patient and attentive.

Dachshunds can also be found on the Internet and in the classified sections of newspapers. Be very careful when buying from these sources, however. Breeders who need to advertise in this way are not always reputable or knowledgeable.

FINDING A RESPONSIBLE BREEDER
Dachshund breeders are not hard to find. There are probably several

QUESTIONS TO ASK A BREEDER

To make sure a breeder is truly committed to breeding and raising healthy Dachshunds, prospective buyers should ask a range of questions. The following list is a good starting point for anyone who is searching for the perfect dog:

How many different breeds do you work with? *The best breeders usually concentrate on one or two breeds.*

How long have you been breeding Dachshunds? *There is no wrong answer, but longer is always better.*

Why did you decide to start breeding Dachshunds? *The answer should not be "for the money."*

Are you familiar with the Dachshund breed standard? *The answer should definitely be* yes. *Breeders who are not familiar with the standard cannot choose the best dams or sires.*

How often is the dam bred? *More than once each year is a huge no-no among responsible breeders.*

How old is the dam? *She should be at least two years old.*

How did you choose the sire? *The sire should be chosen based on looks and temperament.*

Were genetic tests performed on the parents? *The answer should be yes. Responsible breeders always have parents tested for problems that could be passed on to puppies.*

How far back can you trace the parents' bloodlines? *The farther the better.*

breeders in your state. But although many people breed Dachshunds, not all of these breeders are reputable. Some breeders are more concerned about making money than they are about the welfare of their dogs or the overall good of the breed.

Good breeders, on the other hand, are dedicated to breeding healthy, well-adjusted Dachshunds and placing them into good homes. They always have the dam (mother) and sire (father) tested for genetic problems prior to breeding, and they do not hesitate to take their puppies to the vet when necessary. Good breeders are also willing to help new owners with problems that may occur after purchase. Expect a reputable breeder to ask you questions about your family and daily life, so that the breeder can match her Dachshunds with the right homes.

When looking for a reputable breeder in your area, ask your veterinarian or check with members of a local or regional Dachshund club. The Dachshund Club of America

Will I be able to meet the parents? *You should be able to meet at least one of them, if not both.*

Where do you raise your puppies? *The best answer is "in my house."*

Do you socialize the puppies? *The answer should be yes. Lack of socialization can lead to serious behavioral problems later on.*

Are your puppies vaccinated? *Puppies should have their initial inoculations before being released to their new owners.*

Have the puppies been checked for parasites? *All Dachshund puppies should be checked and treated for worms and other parasites after they are weaned.*

How much will a puppy cost? *There is no wrong answer to this. Expect to pay a significant sum if you are buying from a good breeder.*

How long will I have to wait for a puppy? *Reputable breeders often have waiting lists. It is not unusual to have to wait several months for a purebred Dachshund pup.*

What is your return policy? *Most reputable breeders will take a puppy back if there is a health problem or compatibility issue.*

Will you be available to answer questions after I take the puppy? *The answer should be yes.*

After answering questions, most breeders will make a few inquiries of their own. Some of the things they will want to know include why you want a dog, what you intend to do with the dog, and how you plan to care for the dog. It is important to answer these questions openly and honestly. Reputable breeders don't want to be intrusive or nosy. They just want to make sure their puppies are going to good homes.

offers a state-by-state directory of breeders at its Web site, www.dachs-hund-dca.org/kennelads.html.

ADOPTING A DACHSHUND

Dachshunds can also be found through shelters, adoption centers, and rescue organizations. In most cases, the procedure for adoption is similar to purchasing a dog from a breeder. There will be a purchase price, which typically will not exceed $100. Some shelters will offer a discount to buyers who are willing to spay or neuter the dog they take home.

Workers at the shelter will probably ask lots of questions to determine whether or not your home and lifestyle are suitable for a pet. Specific inquiries may include questions about your work schedule, living situation, or history with other pets. Although shelters rarely turn people away, most do reserve the right to reject applications at their discretion.

DESIRABLE DACHSHUND CHARACTERISTICS

Whether you buy a Dachshund from a breeder or adopt an older dog, it helps to know what characteristics to look for. First and foremost, you want a dog that's healthy and in good condition. Taking on a sick pup can

be expensive, and may even lead to heartbreak if the animal has a serious illness that your vet cannot treat successfully.

While a veterinary checkup is really the only way to confirm that your pet has no physical problems, you can get a good idea about a Dachshund's overall condition if you look him over carefully yourself. To start, make sure there's no discharge from his eyes, nose, or ears. Then, check his skin and coat. Both should appear healthy and free of parasites. Scabs, rashes, or bald spots may mean that the Dachshund has some sort of infection or skin problem. Dark specks that move around on the coat or fall off when the dog is petted or brushed are a sign of fleas or another parasite.

Next, watch how a prospective pet Dachshund moves. An awkward gait or short, choppy movements may indicate a serious physical problem. You'll also want to look at his

FAST FACT

The adoption process can take more than a day to complete. Shelters often need several days to review an application and complete all of the necessary paperwork.

build to make sure the dog is neither too thin nor too heavy. Excessive scrawniness may be due to a parasite or illness. It can also be a sign that the dog is underfed and malnourished. If his belly is swollen, it may be because it's full of worms. A veterinarian can easily treat this problem; however, it does take time to get rid of worms and there is a chance that the parasites may cause

some other physical problem that is more difficult to cure.

Just because a dog is healthy doesn't mean that he is the right choice for you. Every dog has a different temperament. If you don't find a Dachshund whose personality matches your lifestyle, you'll be sorry later. For example, if you have children, you'll want a good-natured and energetic pet that can hold his own in

QUESTIONS TO ASK A SHELTER

Here are some suggested questions that a prospective buyer can ask during the adoption process to determine whether or not a particular dog from a shelter or rescue organization would be a good choice:

Was this dog a stray, a rescue, or owner surrender? *There is no wrong answer; it is important to learn more about the dog and his circumstances.*

Has the dog been examined by a veterinarian? *Ideally, the answer should be yes.*

Has the dog been vaccinated? *The answer should be yes unless the dog is too young to have received all of his inoculations.*

Has the dog been checked for internal parasites? *The answer should be yes.*

Does the dog have any known health con-

ditions? *Ideally, the answer should be no; if it is yes, ask for an explanation of the condition and its prognosis.*

Has the dog received a socialization check-up or temperament evaluation? *There is no wrong answer to this question, but it is good to ask so that you can learn more about the dog.*

Is the dog friendly toward other animals? *The answer to this question should be yes, especially if you have another pet at home.*

Has the dog received any training while at the shelter? *There is no wrong answer. Some shelters teach dogs basic commands; others do not.*

What is your return policy? *Most shelters, centers, and organizations will take a dog back if there is a serious health problem or compatibility issue.*

a variety of situations. On the other hand, if you have a laid-back lifestyle and no little ones, a more easygoing dog could be the better choice.

If you're adopting an older dog, you'll get a pretty good idea of what his personality and temperament will be like just by watching him for a little while. But it's hard to determine exactly how a puppy will look or act when he grows up. Before purchasing a puppy, watch how he interacts with his littermates. Observing a puppy's parents will also give you a good idea of what the pup will look and act like as an adult.

Regardless of what you may have heard, don't let a puppy pick you. If you choose the brash puppy that runs up to you first, and isn't afraid to step on the heads of his brothers and sisters to get close to you and catch your attention, you're liable to end up with a pushy pet that's difficult to control. At the same time, if you pick the puppy that hangs back and shows no interest in you, you may end up with a shy and distrustful dog that eventually turns on you or on someone else out of fear. Such dogs can be hard to bring out of their shell. If you're a novice dog owner, the challenge may be too much to handle. The safe bet is to choose a puppy that falls somewhere in the middle. In other words, look for a pup that is neither too dominant nor too submissive when playing with his littermates.

If you're working with a breeder, be sure to ask about the puppies' temperaments. Often, a breeder will suggest which puppy she thinks will be a good fit for you. In some cases the breeder will choose the puppy for you.

CHAPTER FOUR

Responsible Dachshund Ownership

Owning a dog is a huge responsibility. It will be your job to nurture and protect your pet. You must make sure your Dachshund is happy and healthy throughout his life. But there are other basic responsibilities associated with dog ownership that you'll need to keep in mind. For example, it's up to you to make sure your Dachshund doesn't become a nuisance to others. Your neighbors will become very angry and may even call the police if you allow your Dachshund to bark constantly, eliminate on other people's yards, damage their property, or growl at neighborhood children. When these kinds of things happen,

Be responsible when walking your Dachshund. Keep him on a leash at all times, and clean up after him immediately if he makes a mess in a public area.

you can't blame the dog—as the owner, these problems are your fault.

IDENTIFICATION

Dachshunds love to investigate and pursue things. This habit, along with their bold and curious nature, can get them into trouble. Many a Dachshund has been lost because he wandered away from his yard and the people who found him were unable to identify him. At minimum, every Dachshund needs a collar with a tag that includes the owner's name and telephone number. Providing this information ensures that the people who find your lost dog will be able to contact you and return him promptly.

Other identification options include more permanent techniques like tattooing and microchip implantation. Both procedures can be performed at your local veterinary clinic, and neither is particularly painful.

Tattooing is the older of the two techniques. If you choose this method of permanent identification, your dog will have a series of numbers tattooed on his body. The inside of the thigh is the most common spot on Dachshunds, as less hair grows there. However, other areas—from the belly to the insides of the ears—can be marked as well. The tattooed ID number might contain

FAST FACT

Printing the statement "needs medication" on a dog's identification tag can encourage the prompt return of a lost or stolen pet.

your telephone number or your dog's AKC registration number.

Although owners have been tattooing their dogs for years, there are some drawbacks to using this identification technique. The tattoo may fade or become unreadable over time, which means it may have to be redone. Another problem is that there are several different organizations that register dog tattoos. You'll need to register your dog and list your contact information with each one as soon as the tattoo is finished.

Microchip implantation is a more modern permanent identification technique. The microchip is actually a computer chip, about the size of a

FAST FACT

Tattooing your Dachshund may deter professional dog thieves. Most dog brokers and laboratories will not buy tattooed animals.

grain of rice, that is implanted in your dog painlessly via an injection. Each chip includes a unique number, so if your Dachshund does get lost or stolen, and is brought to a veterinarian clinic or shelter anywhere in North America, the staff should be able to scan the dog's back with a special microchip reader. Your contact information will come up, and you'll be contacted and reunited with your pet.

You can probably find information on the Internet about your municipality's regulations and restrictions on dog ownership.

The major drawback to microchip implantation is that there are several chips and scanners on the market, and not all of them are compatible. There have also been reports of some chips moving around in the body, as opposed to staying in the spot where they were first implanted. If that happens, a microchip scanner may not pick up the implanted information.

The best solution is to use two forms of identification for your pet. If your Dachshund has a tag and a tattoo, a tattoo and a microchip, or a microchip and a tag, the chances of being reunited with your missing pet are much greater.

LICENSING REQUIREMENTS

Every municipality in the United States requires pet owners to register their dogs. In most cases, an annual license must be purchased. You can usually get a license from your local courthouse. In some states, you may be able to purchase a license directly from your veterinarian.

The fee for licensing your Dachshund will vary, depending on where you live and other factors. Typically, the cost will range from $5 to $50. Some cities will offer a lower fee if you have spayed or neutered your pet, or if your dog has permanent identification, like a tattoo or a microchip.

If you fail to get a license for your Dachshund, you'll probably be subject to a stiff fine. In some areas, not licensing your dog is considered a misdemeanor offense. To save yourself any trouble, you should abide by the law and purchase the appropriate license for your dog each year.

COMMON LEGAL ISSUES

Failure to purchase a dog license isn't the only thing that can get pet owners into trouble with the law. Barking and trespassing Dachshunds can also create legal issues for their owners. By nature, Dachshunds are vocal animals—these dogs were originally bred to bark loudly when they trapped prey underground, so their owners could hear them and dig up the prey. Unfortunately, many pet Dachshunds consider it their duty to make as much noise as possible when they see a passing car, person, or another animal. Even the smartest Dachshund will not understand why neighbors don't appreciate this sort of behavior.

It is up to owners to make sure their barking pets do not break noise ordinances or become a nuisance to neighbors. Violating a noise ordinance or allowing a dog to trespass on a neighbor's property can result in a citation or a fine. If multiple violations occur, a magistrate may force an owner to give up her pet.

Not picking up after your Dachshund can also get you into hot water. If you're walking your dog, bring plastic bags along and be sure to clean up any messes he might leave behind. The fines for not doing so can be considerable.

WHEN YOUR DACHSHUND BITES

According to the U.S. Centers for Disease Control and Prevention, dogs bite more than 4.7 million people in the United States each year. Medical treatment is required in

Don't allow a barking Dachshund puppy or adult to annoy your neighbors.

Warning visitors to your home that you own a dog can help prevent bites.

more than 800,000 cases. Half of the people treated are children.

If your Dachshund is aggressive, you must take precautions to make sure nobody gets bitten. Keep your dog away from children, post signs on your property, and warn visitors about potential danger the moment they enter your house or yard. You may also want to seek out a trainer or behavior specialist to find out how you can control or correct your pet's biting or aggressive behavior.

It's your responsibility to make sure that your Dachshund does not bite a person or another animal. If he does, you'll be held responsible. The legal ramifications can be serious and, depending on the severity of the bite, expensive. According to data provided by the Insurance Information Institute, the insurance payout for the average dog bite claim is more than $24,000.

SPAYING OR NEUTERING YOUR DACHSHUND

Unless you plan to show or breed your Dachshund, spaying (females) or neutering (males) your pet is the responsible thing to do. Every year, thousands of unwanted dogs are abandoned at shelters and pounds. Many of these dogs are never adopted, and are eventually put to death. Spaying or neutering your pet will make sure your Dachshund doesn't contribute to the pet over-population problem by preventing unwanted puppies.

FAST FACT

Many homeowner's insurance policies, and even some renter's policies, cover dog bite liability. If you own a dog, check your policy to make sure you're covered in the event he bites someone. If you're not covered by your current insurance policy, you can purchase umbrella insurance or dog liability insurance from a number of carriers that specialize in liability or pet insurance coverage.

A lesser-known benefit is that spaying or neutering will help your pet live a longer and healthier life. Females that have been spayed are not susceptible to uterine or ovarian cancer, and are less likely to develop breast cancer. Males that have been neutered will not develop testicular cancer and are less likely to suffer from prostate disease.

Dachshunds can be spayed or neutered at six months of age. Most vets suggest spaying a female before her first heat cycle. Both surgeries are relatively inexpensive and can be performed in the veterinarian's office. If properly medicated, your Dachshund will experience minimal pain. However, some vets may require spayed or neutered puppies to stay in the clinic for a day or two to recover from the surgery.

Don't worry that this procedure will change your pet for the worse. It's a myth that sterilizing a dog changes his temperament or personality. Spaying or neutering your Dachshund will make your dog a better, more affectionate pet, and will almost always eliminate unwanted behaviors, like aggression and roaming.

PET INSURANCE

To cover the cost of medical procedures, such as spaying and neutering, some people purchase pet insurance policies. Pet insurance has been available for more than two decades, and is becoming more popular as growing numbers of pet owners recognize the importance of good veterinary care.

Most pet insurance plans cover the cost of treatment in case of an accident, illness, or serious medical problem. An increasing number of carriers also provide coverage for

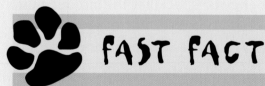

FAST FACT

Some pet insurance plans don't cover congenital and hereditary conditions associated with the Dachshund breed. Ask your pet insurance carrier for a list of exclusions before you purchase a policy.

FAST FACT

Although pet insurance plans can be a smart financial investment for some people, they do not pay off for everyone. In fact, it may cost more to pay the insurance premiums, deductibles, and co-pays than it does to simply pay for veterinary care.

preventative care, such as annual checkups, teeth cleaning, heartworm and flea control, spaying or neutering, and some health screenings, such as testing for parasites. The policies that include preventative care coverage tend to cost a little more, so do the math to make sure the insurance plan makes financial sense for you.

Dozens of companies offer health insurance plans for pets, as do organizations like the American Society for the Prevention of Cruelty to Animals (ASPCA) and the American Kennel Club. However, every pet insurance plan is different, so it's a good idea to research and compare several plans before making a final decision. Specific things to compare include the level of coverage being offered, monthly or annual rates, co-pays, deductibles, and the method by which insurance carriers pay claims. Some will pay your veterinarian directly, while others require you to pay upfront, fill out a claim form, and get reimbursed at a later date. Comparing all of these factors will help pet owners choose the most appropriate pet insurance policy.

CHAPTER FIVE

The Best Possible Beginning

Bringing home a Dachshund is a lot like bringing home a new-born baby. The house and the family must be prepared for the new addition. The first thing a Dachshund will want to do is sniff his new space and meet everyone in it. Creating a safe environment that is full of love will ensure the best possible beginning. This is best done before you bring your new pet home, because once your Dachshund enters the door all eyes will be on him.

PUPPY-PROOFING YOUR HOME

Dachshunds are curious. If a Dachshund really wants something that has been left where he can see

This long-haired Miniature Dachshund is curious about the world outside. Make sure that your pet's curiosity doesn't lead to trouble by eliminating dangers inside and outside your home.

it—be it a shoe, an electrical cord, or a family heirloom—he will generally find a way to get the item. Thus it is essential that potential hazards be removed from each room in the house, so that your Dachshund does not accidentally swallow something dangerous or destroy something valuable.

When looking to remove temptation from under your Dachshund's long nose, start by getting low to the floor. This way, you'll be able to see the world from your pet's perspective. Keep in mind that Dachshunds are small enough to get into relatively confined spaces. Look for anything that can fit inside a Dachshund's mouth, and make sure that it's out of reach.

LIVING ROOM OR FAMILY ROOM:
Dangling electrical cords and window shade strings are usually the most dangerous items in living rooms and family rooms. Every loose cord, string, and tassel should be hidden, taped down, or covered. You may also want to remove remote controls, knick-knacks, and other items that normally sit on coffee tables and other easy-to-reach places.

BEDROOMS:
The typical bedroom contains a variety of potential hazards for a Dachshund. Dogs can easily swallow earrings and necklaces. They have also been known to ingest socks and other small items of clothing. Any of these items can create an obstruction that requires emergency surgery. All clothing—clean and otherwise—should be kept in drawers or behind closed doors, and jewelry should be kept in a box or container that your dog can't reach.

BATHROOMS:
Child locks should be placed on bathroom cabinets to keep nosy puppies away from cleaning supplies, medications, and beauty products. It is also a good idea to keep low countertops free of cosmetics, curling irons, hairdryers, and other items.

KITCHEN:
Like most dogs, Dachshunds love to hang around the kitchen because that's where food can be found. Putting child locks on the cabinets, particularly ones in which food or trash are located, may be the only way to keep this natural

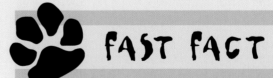

FAST FACT

Pet supply stores sell foul-tasting but non-toxic substances that can be sprayed on furniture and other items to discourage puppies from chewing.

hunter from joyfully cleaning out the pantry or knocking over the garbage can when you're not in the room.

GARAGE: Most garages contain all sorts of hazardous items: antifreeze, cleaning supplies, pesticides, fertilizers, fuels, and other substances that are very toxic to pets. These products should be locked in a cabinet or kept

Garages, utility sheds, and other places where dangerous items like gasoline, paint, electrical cords, or power tools are stored should be off-limits to your Dachshund.

on a high shelf so your Dachshund can't get to them. The same is true of sharp tools and items that are small enough to be swallowed.

Other potential hazards include houseplants, litter boxes, purses, and backpacks. Certain houseplants are toxic to dogs, and will cause serious illness or even death if ingested. Swallowing cat litter can cause a Dachshund to choke or suffer from impacted intestines. Purses and backpacks become dangerous when they contain food, gum, mints, or something else that a dog finds pleasantly smelly. In rummaging around to get the food, your Dachshund may swallow other small items.

PUPPY-PROOFING YOUR YARD

Puppy-proofing your yard is just as important as puppy-proofing your home. Your Dachshund will spend part of every day outside. There are many different things in the average yard that can be chewed or swallowed. Potential hazards include kids' toys and garden tools. These items should be picked up before your Dachshund is allowed to roam freely.

Plants and flowers can also be very dangerous. Azalea, daffodils, baby's breath, mistletoe, holly, English ivy, nightshade and many other common plants are toxic to

Dachshunds. It only takes a few seconds for your dog to eat these deadly plants, so either remove them from your yard or block your Dachshund's access to your garden.

Pools, fences, kennels, and similar structures must also be made secure. An unsupervised puppy could fall into a pool or become entangled within a pool cover. Fences and kennels pose entirely different problems. If the fence or gate isn't sturdy or flush with the ground, a Dachshund may try to wriggle his way out of an enclosure. As he does, he could hurt himself on a jagged piece of fence. If your dog manages to escape, he could wander off into the street, get hit by a car, and end up with far worse than a cut or minor injury.

CREATING A SECURE SPACE FOR YOUR DACHSHUND

Before bringing a puppy home, it is a good idea to decide where the puppy may and may not go within the house. A Dachshund will want to sniff out every inch of his new world

Make sure that your garden does not contain plants that are toxic to dogs. The ASPCA provides a list of poisonous plants on its Web site at www.aspca.org/pet-care/poison-control/plants.

as soon as he arrives. If certain rooms are off-limits, he should know that immediately. You can create solid boundaries by keeping doors closed or installing a gate or other obstruction in entryways.

Many Dachshund owners allow their pet to have the run of the house. There is absolutely nothing wrong with this. Still, it's important to create a small and secure space to help your puppy settle into his new home. This space could be a laundry room, mudroom, or another area with puppy-friendly floors. If your house doesn't have such a room, you can use an exercise pen. These pens are small enough to be placed in any room, but large enough for a puppy to have space to move around and play.

Whenever a puppy is left alone for an extended period, he should be kept in his safe place. This not only provides a sense of security for the puppy, it also prevents him from getting into trouble. Because dogs are pack animals, most puppies do not enjoy being alone. You can reduce your pet's separation anxiety by filling your Dachshund's space with things that interest him, such as a favorite blanket or a fun chew toy. As your Dachshund grows older and learns the rules of the house, you can give him more space to roam when you're away.

Dachshunds typically like to have their own "den" to burrow into when they want to sleep, hide from danger, or just have a little quiet time. A plastic or a wire crate can serve this

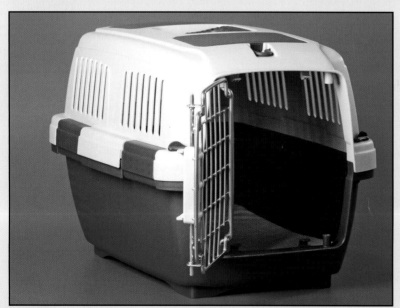

A small plastic or wire crate can serve as a good den for your Dachshund. Crating isn't cruel unless you leave the dog locked up for long periods. You should never leave a Dachshund puppy confined in a crate for more than four hours at a time. During the night, your puppy will need to be allowed out several times to eliminate; his bladder won't be large enough to sleep through the night until he's at least six months old.

purpose very well. The crate should be big enough for your Dachshund to comfortably stand up and turn around. However, it shouldn't be too large. Dogs don't like to urinate where they sleep, so a Dachshund puppy with a large crate will have no problem making a mess in one corner and sleeping in another. For Miniature Dachshunds, a small dog crate (24 inches/61 cm) is ideal; Standard Dachshunds will fit better in a medium-sized crate (30 inches/76 cm).

PREPARING YOUR FAMILY

Preparing your family for the new arrival is just as important as preparing the home. Consistency is the key to raising a happy, healthy Dachshund, so establish ground rules before your puppy arrives. Everyone in the household should sit down together to discuss how to handle common situations. Specific subjects to talk about should include what the puppy will eat, when the puppy will eat, and what steps will be taken to train and socialize the puppy.

Responsibilities should also be assigned before your puppy arrives. Establish who will feed the puppy, who will walk the puppy, and who will be taking time each day to train the puppy. Make sure everyone understands the rules about how the puppy will be treated, as well as their responsibilities.

If there are young children in the house, there should also be a brief education session about proper handling of a pet. A child who plays too rough can easily injure a small dog like a

Young children need to be taught how to properly handle a puppy, and should never be left alone with a pet dog.

Dachshund. It is essential that everyone in the house understand how a puppy should be handled.

BRINGING YOUR DACHSHUND HOME

Before bringing a Dachshund home, try to assemble everything your puppy will need when he arrives. Nothing is worse than being forced to leave your new puppy at home because you forgot to pick up a necessity. Make sure that you have food, dog dishes, a small collar, a leash, a toy for the puppy to play with, and a crate in which to train and transport the puppy. It's also a good idea to have carpet cleaner, stain remover, and other cleaning supplies on hand. Puppies always have accidents during their first few weeks. If not cleaned up properly, the smell will encourage even more accidents.

The final item you will need is a list of last-minute questions to ask the breeder or shelter employees. Make sure you find out the puppy's vaccination schedule, diet, and feeding times. If you are picking up an older dog, you will want to get this information as well as find out about the dog's favorite toys and his ability to follow commands.

It's a good idea for at least two people to make the trip to the breeder or shelter to pick up your

Dachshund. This will enable the driver to concentrate on the road while the passenger or passengers take care of the dog. Taking along a towel and a couple of plastic bags is also smart. There is a good possibility that the puppy will get carsick or have an accident during the trip home. Being able to absorb and clean up the mess will make the ride much more pleasant.

There are two ways to transport your Dachshund: on a passenger's lap or in a pet carrier. Riding on someone's lap can be very comforting for the puppy, but it can also be dangerous. If the vehicle stops suddenly or is involved in an accident, the puppy could fly right out of the person's arms. There is also a chance the puppy could be killed if an airbag deploys during a crash. Although a pet carrier will not do much to reassure a scared puppy, it is a much safer option.

THE FIRST NIGHT

The first time he sets foot in his new home, your Dachshund will be just as excited as you and your family. There will be all sorts of interesting new sights, sounds, and scents for him to explore. Give your new pup a few minutes to investigate his surroundings. Once he's had time to check things out, and maybe take a bathroom break, he will be ready to meet everyone in the family. Introductions should be made slowly and kindly. The puppy will feel much less overwhelmed if he gets to meet everyone in turn instead of all at once. Next, show your Dachshund where his bed, food and water dishes, and chew toys are located.

The next few hours will probably include lots of sniffing, playing, barking, and puppy kisses. At some point, the puppy will probably succumb to exhaustion. This is completely normal. Puppies play hard, but they also spend a lot of time sleeping. If your new pal wants to take a nap, let him. He might not get very much sleep when night finally rolls around.

A puppy's first night in a new place is often rough, particularly if the puppy is used to sleeping with littermates. The experience of being alone at night can be very traumatic. To let everyone know how much he's suffering, the puppy may cry and whine for hours on end. His goal is to attract someone who is willing to comfort and play with him. Whatever you do, don't fall for it. It's okay to get up several times to let the puppy outside the first night, but you shouldn't get up just to comfort him. If you do, he'll learn that crying and whining are the best ways to get attention throughout the night.

If you want to make things easier on your puppy, and reassure him, put his crate in your bedroom. Sometimes just being able to see someone else is all a puppy needs to settle down and fall asleep. You can also put a hot water bottle or a piece of bedding from his former home in the crate to offer warmth or the comforting scent of something familiar.

YOUR DACHSHUND'S FIRST YEAR

The first few months with your Dachshund will be both fun and challenging. You'll enjoy watching your little dog grow, and take pride as he learns new skills. He'll surely provide many memories that you'll laugh over and cherish later. Of course, there will also be times when you find yourself wondering why you ever wanted a dog.

Remember, your Dachshund puppy will look to you for love and guidance. No matter what you are feeling, be patient with your pet and

Puppies will become confused if you allow a behavior one day but not the next. Apply rules in a consistent way, and your pet will learn right from wrong faster.

provide him with the affection and training he'll need to grow into a happy, healthy, and well-adjusted dog. If you remain loving and consistent in your training throughout the first few months, you will eventually end up with a well-behaved and devoted companion.

Until that day, encourage good behavior by developing routines that your Dachshund can follow. This will help both of you adjust to your new life together. Some of the activities that should always be done on a regular schedule include feedings, walks, and bathroom breaks. You should also work on obedience training each day.

As you are working and bonding with your Dachshund, you'll probably notice dramatic changes in his behavior from week to week. This is normal. Dogs change as they become more accustomed to their surround-

ings. Age can also have an impact on behavior and development.

The rate at which a Dachshund puppy's behavior matures can vary. A dog's cognitive development often depends on genetics and environment as well as the puppy's size—some puppies grow into adulthood faster than others. However, there are some milestones every owner can count on. This growth and cognitive development schedule offers an indication of what you can expect during your Dachshund's first year of life:

BIRTH TO SEVEN WEEKS: Like other dogs, Dachshunds are born without sight or a sense of smell. They depend on their mothers for food and warmth during the first two weeks of life. Sleep is their main priority, but most puppies will respond to gentle touching. After this, over the next five weeks, Dachshund puppies develop motor skills, vision, and hearing. They also begin to interact more with their mother and littermates. This is the time when they learn how to function within a pack. Most Dachshund puppies realize during this period that they can bark and make other noises to express themselves.

EIGHT TO TWELVE WEEKS: By eight weeks of age, a Dachshund puppy's

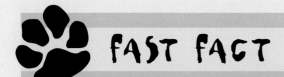

FAST FACT

Showing your new Dachshund off around the neighborhood can be fun but it can also be dangerous. Dachshund puppies are very susceptible to viruses, parasites, and bacteria. Travel and socialization with other animals should always be kept to a minimum until the puppy has been wormed and vaccinated.

During their first few weeks of life, Dachshund puppies are blind and spend most of their time sleeping.

brain is fully developed. The puppy should be starting to socialize with humans. He should also be weaned and fully aware of where his food and water dishes are located. Typically, a breeder will not allow you to take a puppy until he has reached this stage.

THIRTEEN TO SIXTEEN WEEKS:

Dachshunds between thirteen and sixteen weeks are considered adolescents. They are much more receptive to basic commands, but they also like to test boundaries. At this age, Dachshund pups begin to associate praise and punishment with certain behaviors.

SEVENTEEN WEEKS TO SIX MONTHS:

Dominant personality traits are fully established during this period. At six months of age, a Dachshund reaches sexual maturity. At this point, puppies should be housebroken and able to understand basic commands, such as "sit," "stay," "down," and "come."

Six Months to One Year: This is the final growing stage for most Dachshunds. By the time Dachshunds are a year old, they have grown almost as large as they will get. At this point, your Dachshund should be fully assimilated into the household.

SOCIALIZATION

The term "socialization" is used to describe the process of introducing a dog to the people, animals, and environment around him. Properly socializing a puppy during his first year is one of the most important things a dog owner can do to ensure

PUPPY SOCIALIZATION TIPS

According to the Cornell University College of Veterinary Medicine, the optimal time for socializing a Dachshund lasts until the puppy is about 12 weeks old. These socialization tips will help you make the most of this crucial period:

- Try to introduce your puppy to new people and experiences gradually so that he is not overwhelmed.
- Ask new people to squat, sit, or kneel so that they don't seem so intimidating to your puppy the first time he meets them.
- Get your puppy used to grooming, riding in the car, walking on a leash, and other experiences he will be participating in on a regular basis.
- Introduce your puppy to new sounds from a distance so that he has no reason to be alarmed.
- Feed your puppy snacks and pet him near items that are commonly considered frightening, such as a vacuum, so that he associates them with good experiences.

- Always be gentle and affectionate with your puppy. If you're not, he may end up being scared of you.
- Don't coddle your puppy when he acts afraid of something. Coddling encourages fearful behavior.
- Don't force a puppy to approach something that frightens him. Doing so could frighten him more and create a lifelong phobia.
- Make sure that other people treat your dog respectfully. Just one bad experience could be enough to undermine your hard work.
- Reward your puppy when he reacts positively to a new experience.
- Do your best to make every new experience positive for your puppy.

Adequate socialization is very important for Dachshund puppies. If you don't have children of your own, invite relatives' children or neighbors' children over for supervised play dates with your Dachshund.

that her pet grows into a dog with a good temperament. The reason for socialization training is to help your pup discover that the world is a friendly place, for the most part, and that the people, animals, and situations he will encounter are interesting but generally harmless.

The most critical time for socialization is during the first twelve weeks of a dog's life. This is when puppies form their impression of the world. Positive experiences will give your Dachshund a positive outlook on life. Negative experiences, on the other hand, can make him a shy, distrustful dog.

Typically, the breeder will start the puppy's socialization. Once you bring your Dachshund puppy home, however, it's up to you to continue the process. After your Dachshund has met everyone in your household, continue introducing him to several

SOCIALIZATION CLASSES

Studies have shown that puppies that attend socialization classes are often better adjusted and more obedient than other dogs. Socialization classes, also known as puppy socials or puppy kindergarten, provide a fun and friendly way for puppies to meet and play with one another. These classes are great for owners who want to introduce their puppies to other dogs in a safe environment.

Puppy socialization classes are often held at obedience schools, vet offices, animal clinics, dog parks, and other places where puppies are welcome. The cost of classes can vary. Rules are also different from class to class.

Your breeder or veterinarian will probably be able to recommend a local socialization class. The best classes will not enroll unvaccinated or aggressive puppies in an attempt to keep things safe and comfortable for everyone involved. Asking about this policy, as well as other rules and procedures, can help you choose the best socialization class for your Dachshund.

new people each week. The more human contact a puppy has, the more likely he is to be comfortable around people in the future. Make sure the people he meets are friendly and gentle, and don't let them do anything that frightens him.

As part of the socialization process, puppies and young dogs should be allowed to meet other animals, such as friendly dogs and cats. You'll also want your pup exposed to many different situations and experiences, so that things like trips to the veterinarian and rides in the car become less scary for him. If properly socialized, Dachshund puppies will grow into happy, healthy adult dogs that love people and tolerate other animals.

CHAPTER SIX

Nutrition, Exercise, Grooming, and Training

During the first few weeks of their lives, Dachshunds receive all of the nutrition they need from their mothers. Puppies nurse every two or three hours for three to four weeks. Most breeders will start weaning Dachshund pups off their mother's milk at this time. Puppies must become accustomed to eating solid food before they can go to their new homes. Breeders usually make this change gradually, so that the

For optimal health, a Dachshund will require at least one 10 to 15 minute walk each day.

puppy's stomach will not get too upset. While being weaned, the puppy is allowed to nurse several times each day, but is also encouraged to eat a gruel-like mixture of ground kibble or meat combined with water or milk. As each week passes, the breeder mixes in more kibble and makes less of an effort to grind up the solid food. Generally, by the time puppies are eight weeks old they are fully weaned and eating puppy food exclusively.

PROPER NUTRITION

When you pick up your puppy from a breeder or shelter, you'll probably be given a bag of food to take with you, or at least a recommendation as to what you should feed the puppy. For the first few days, it is best to continue the food choice and the feeding schedule chosen by the breeder. This will ensure that the puppy is getting the right amount of food for his age and size. If you change the puppy's diet or don't feed him at his regularly scheduled times, he will almost certainly get an upset tummy.

After a few days, you can gradually introduce a different brand of food into your Dachshund's diet. Start by mixing in a few tablespoons of the new food with each feeding. Then, add more and more of the new food and less and less of the old over the next two weeks until each meal consists of nothing but the new food you have chosen.

Whatever brand of dog food that you select, be sure to check the label on the package. If it does not include the American Association of Food Control Officials (AAFCO) stamp of approval, then the food almost certainly does not contain the appropriate amount of vitamins and minerals

"Free feeding," or leaving food out for your dog to nibble on during the day, is not a good practice. Instead, set out his meals at the same times each day, and remove uneaten food after 20 to 25 minutes. Your dog should always have fresh water available, though.

for your pet. You'll also want to take a close look at the ingredient list. Some kind of meat should be the first ingredient. Foods that have a grain or corn base are not as good for your puppy's health. Puppies need protein and fatty acids for energy and to build muscles and connective tissue, so look for a dry food that has been specially formulated for puppies.

At your first visit to the veterinarian, discuss your dog's diet. Your vet can recommend several brands of food that would be appropriate for your Dachshund, and will also be able to advise you on the best feeding schedule as your puppy grows. Dried kibble is almost always recommended for Dachshunds. This type of food has less fat, less sugar, and in many cases, more nutrients than canned or semi-moist food. Dried kibble is also less expensive and can help to control and reduce the amount of tartar that accumulates on a dog's teeth.

FEEDING SCHEDULES

Dachshunds have an unrivaled appetite for food. If allowed to eat as much as they want, whenever they want, they will become eating machines. This is not only expensive but also dangerous. Free feeding (leaving food out 24 hours per day) can lead to obesity, which will in turn lead to other health problems. The best way to avoid this is by establishing a regular feeding schedule.

Feeding Schedule for Puppies
Young Dachshund puppies should eat at least four small meals daily—one in the morning, two in the afternoon, and one at night. Each meal should be nutritionally complete and given at approximately the same time each day. At six months of age, Dachshunds only need to be fed three times each day—once in the morning, once at noon, and once at night.

Feeding Schedule for Adult Dogs
Adult dogs don't need to eat as frequently as puppies. At 10 to 12 months of age, a Dachshund's feedings can be reduced to once or twice per day. Feedings can occur in the morning or at night. If the Dachshund is fed twice daily, he should eat the first meal in the morning and the second at night.

Feeding Schedule for Senior Dogs
A senior dog's dietary needs may change, but in most cases there is no reason to deviate from the feeding schedule for an adult dog. At most, senior dogs need to eat twice a day.

Owners who would prefer to feed their Dachshund a more natural diet may consider making meals themselves. Low-fat, homemade food diets can provide all of the nutrition a growing puppy needs. However, the diet must be formatted correctly to ensure puppies ingest the correct portion to provide the protein and nutrients they need for healthy growth. Your vet should be able to recommend portion sizes and help you devise a tasty yet balanced diet for your pet.

As Dachshunds grow and age, their dietary needs may change. Young, active adult dogs need more food than older, sedentary dogs that spend the bulk of their time on the couch. Dogs also have different nutrition requirements as they grow older. Adult Dachshunds need protein to build and strengthen muscles and fats for energy and to keep their skin and coat healthy. Carbohydrates and fiber are also important in the proper quantities. As your Dachshund ages, your veterinarian will help you address the dog's changing dietary needs.

EXERCISE

If you don't exercise your Dachshund properly, it won't matter how careful you are about his diet—he will be unhealthy and possibly obese. Obesity can lead to a whole host of health problems and may take years off your dog's life. To keep your Dachshund in good condition, make sure he exercises regularly.

Originally, Dachshunds were bred to be active hunters. These dogs had to be nimble and hardy enough to chase badgers and other small game into holes in the ground. Although today's Dachshunds are much less likely to participate in such activities, they still enjoy brisk daily walks. Walking will help your pet exercise his limbs and keep his heart strong. Ten to 15 minutes is usually sufficient, though most Dachshunds will be happy to walk longer. They love to sniff out new trails and take in the sights and sounds.

Fetch is a game that your Dachshund can enjoy inside or outside. Running through the house or around your fenced yard in pursuit of a favorite ball or toy will keep your Dachshund fit and entertained. Playing fetch will also bring joy to

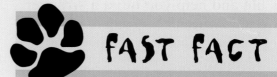

FAST FACT

A sudden change in a puppy's diet can result in an upset stomach or diarrhea. Diarrhea can dehydrate a Dachshund puppy in just a few hours.

also make sure your dog stays hydrated with plenty of fresh water.

GROOMING

Smooth Dachshunds and Wirehaired Dachshunds do not require a lot of grooming to appear their best. With either of these varieties, you'll have to brush your dog's coat about once a week to keep it looking shiny and free of mats. A soft bristle brush or grooming glove works well on Smooth Dachshunds. Wirehaired Dachshunds can be combed and brushed using both a bristle brush and a slicker brush or fine-toothed grooming comb. Regular brushing will help to control shedding, as the slicker brush will remove loose hairs from your Wirehaired Dachshund's undercoat. For Wirehaired Dachshunds, special care should be taken to remove mats, tangles, dirt, and debris. This will keep your Dachshund's skin healthier and will make his coat easier to wash.

A Longhaired Dachshund should be brushed every other day using a slicker brush. Pay particular attention to the long, fine hairs that hang from the legs and sides. This hair tends to pick up dirt and debris, and is prone to mats and tangles. Use a fine-toothed grooming comb to clean this hair and prevent mats from forming. After brushing a Longhaired

Dachshunds are energetic and playful dogs, and typically will enjoy playing ball with their owners at any time.

his life and help you build a stronger bond with your pet.

No matter what exercise you choose, it is important to keep an eye on your pet the entire time. Dachshunds can overdo it when they are having fun. If your dog looks tired or hurt, you should stop the exercise immediately. You should

Dachshund, use grooming scissors to trim the long hairs at the end of his tail, ears, legs, and feet.

Try to be as gentle as possible during brushing sessions. Brushing too hard can scratch a Dachshund's skin. Make an effort to brush in the direction that his hair is growing. This will not only loosen and remove dead hair, it also will relax your Dachshund by making him feel he's being petted.

Dachshunds don't need baths often. In fact, frequent bathing can dry out a Dachshund's skin, making him feel itchy. If you brush your Dachshund properly, he'll only need a bath about every other month. You may, however, need to bathe your pet any time that he's rolled in something particularly smelly or sticky.

BATHING: When you do wash your Dachshund, be gentle and sensitive to his feelings. Most dogs would prefer to avoid baths. Bathing can be less stressful for all involved if you have the right equipment on hand

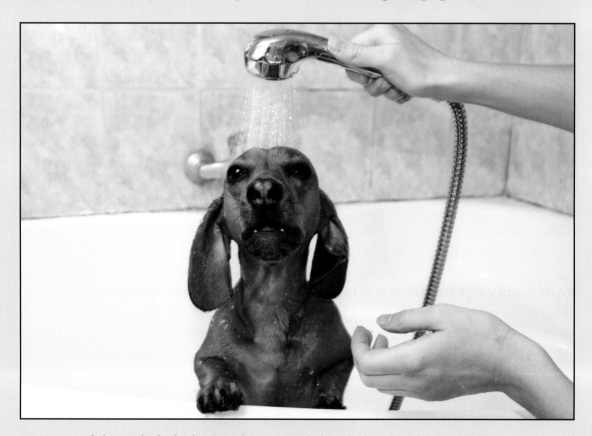

Waiting until the end of a bath to wash your Dachshund's head and face will keep you drier during the bathing process. Once your dog's head gets wet, he'll want to shake off the water.

When the bath is finished, dry your Dachshund's coat with a soft towel. Because most dogs don't care for baths, your caring touch afterward will seem like an extra reward.

before you start. You'll need a tub that is large enough for your Dachshund to sit and stand in comfortably. Because Dachshunds are so small, they can be bathed in a laundry tub or even the kitchen sink. Regardless of where you do it, you'll most definitely need a hose or spray attachment to rinse out shampoo. A non-slip rubber mat for the bottom of the tub will give your pet good traction, so he won't hurt himself by slipping and sliding. You'll also want

to bring cotton balls, dog shampoo, a few treats, and towels for drying.

Start by placing your dog in the unfilled tub, and placing cotton balls in his ears so that water doesn't get into his ear canals. Wet down his coat with lukewarm water, using the shower hose or a plastic pitcher. Try not to get your Dachshund's head wet—once a dog's head gets wet, he will want to shake off the water. Dilute a quarter-cup of the dog shampoo in about a gallon of warm water; this will make the soap easier to work into and rinse out of your Dachshund's coat. Apply the diluted shampoo and lather it through the coat, starting at the neck and working toward the tail. Lather your dog's head last, being very careful not to get shampoo or water in your Dachshund's eyes, ears, or nose. You can use a soft cloth and warm water to gently wash his face.

When you're done, rinse the soap out of his coat, starting with the head and working toward his tail. Be sure to thoroughly rinse out all the shampoo. Any residue that remains in his coat will attract dirt, make his coat feel sticky, and cause dry, itchy skin. Once the coat has been rinsed clean, you can hand-dry your Dachshund using a soft, fluffy towel. For Longhaired Dachshunds, squeeze excess water out of the coat with a towel, then thoroughly dry your pet with a blow dryer. Make sure to use the lowest heat setting so you don't irritate his skin.

Throughout the bathing process, praise and encourage your dog to relax him, and dole out treats periodically to reward good behavior in the tub. Brush or comb your dog's hair immediately after bathing.

NAIL CARE: Nail care is an important part of a Dachshund's regular grooming routine. On average, a Dachshund's nails will need to be

Regularly trimming your Dachshund's nails will cause the quick, the blood supply in the nail, to recede. This will enable you to keep his nails short. If you're not sure where the quick is, err on the side of caution. It is better to leave your dog's nails a little long than to cut the blood vessel, as this will cause pain and bleeding.

FAST FACT

Dogs don't enjoy having their nails clipped, but you can get your Dachshund accustomed to the procedure if you start early. When he's a puppy, touch his paws frequently, rubbing the nails gently with your fingers. This will get him used to having his nails touched. Showing him a pair of nail clippers every now and then during treat time won't hurt either.

trimmed at least once a month. More frequent nail trims may be required for your pet if his nails grow unusually fast. A good rule of thumb is, if you can hear a dog's nails clicking when he walks on a wood, linoleum, or tile floor, his nails are too long.

To trim your dog's nails at home, you will need a pair of nail clippers that are specially made for dogs. It is also essential to have a blood clotting agent, such as a styptic pencil or styptic powder, on hand. If the nail is cut too short, it will bleed profusely until a clotting agent has been applied.

Begin by supporting the dog's paw and selecting a toe, then look for the quick—the blood vessels and nerves inside the nail. The quick will look like a line running through the center of the nail that doesn't quite

reach the tip. On dark or black nails, the quick can be hard to see, but it must be avoided. If you can't see the quick, clip slowly and carefully. Trim off little bits at a time until you are sure of the quick's location. If you cut too deep, you'll nick the blood vessels, causing bleeding and pain. In that case, apply the styptic powder or other coagulant to stop the bleeding. Be sure to speak to your Dachshund in a soothing voice throughout the procedure so that he is put at ease. When you're finished, give him a treat and lots of praise.

If you don't feel confident using sharp clippers on your dog's nails, you can file them down by hand instead. Pet supply stores sell convex files specially designed for this purpose. Another option, if you're willing to pay a fee, is to have a groomer or veterinarian perform this task.

EAR CARE: A Dachshund's long, hanging ears provide the ideal breeding ground for bacteria and fungi. They are also a magnet for *Otodectes cynotis*, a type of mite that lives in dogs' ear canals. If ears aren't checked and cleaned regularly, Dachshunds can develop infections. Infections will make the dog's ears smelly, and can also cause itching and pain. If left untreated, some infections can lead to permanent hearing

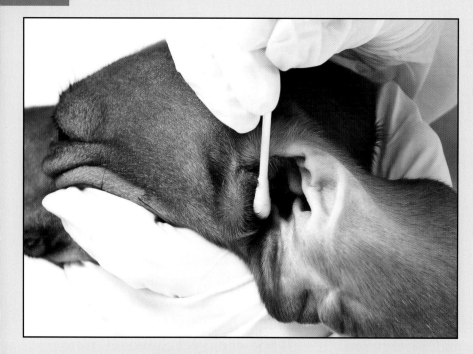

You can use a cotton swab to clean dirt and wax from the exterior of your Dachshund's ears. However, never insert any object into your dog's ear canal. If you see an object that you can't flush away with cleaning solution, ask your veterinarian to remove it.

loss. You can catch infections early, and possibly avoid them altogether, by checking and cleaning your Dachshund's ears on a regular basis.

Ear cleaning solutions can be purchased from a veterinarian or pet supply store. These solutions usually contain a mixture of water and vinegar. They are ideal for cleaning but are not medicated. If you think your dog has an ear infection or ear mites, you should take him to the vet immediately so that you can get a medicated solution and, if necessary, antibiotics to fight the infection.

Before checking or cleaning your Dachshund's ears, be prepared for plenty of squirming. Most dogs do not enjoy having their ears cleaned. The cleaning solution is usually cold-er than the dog's body temperature. This can cause slight discomfort as well as a tickling sensation. If necessary, get someone to help you hold your Dachshund still so that you can do the job properly.

Begin by visually inspecting your dog's ears. Some dirt and wax is to be expected. But if you see an excessive amount of either, there could be a problem. The color of the wax can also be an indicator of infection or mites. Wax that is yellow or light brown in color points to a healthy ear. Black or reddish brown wax, on the other hand, is not normal. This is a sign of infection.

Squirt the recommended amount of solution in the dog's ears. Massage the outside of the ear gently to work the solution into all of the crevices. Then, use a cotton ball or cotton swab to carefully clean out any visible wax and dirt from beneath the earflap.

DENTAL CARE: Like humans, dogs can suffer from tartar buildup, cavities, gum disease, and other dental issues. Nearly 80 percent of Dachshunds will show signs of periodontal disease by the age of three if their teeth are not properly treated. Periodontal disease can make it difficult for dogs to chew and may even be fatal if allowed to progress unchecked.

When your puppy is six months old, you should develop a biweekly brushing routine. Plaque will begin to develop on a puppy's permanent teeth at this age and should be removed periodically to avoid buildup. Brushing should be done with a specially formulated doggie toothpaste and toothbrush. These items can be purchased from a pet supply store or veterinarian's office. You should never use human toothpaste to brush a Dachshund's teeth. Human toothpaste is harsh and may upset a dog's stomach.

Always brush your Dachshund's teeth gently using the amount of paste recommended on the tube. Make as many vertical passes with the brush as you can, lifting your dog's lips whenever necessary to get the outer surface of each tooth.

Regular brushing, at least twice a week, will help keep your Dachshund's teeth clean and healthy. Giving your Dachshund appropriate chew toys will also help, as regular chewing will help prevent plaque from building up on dental enamel.

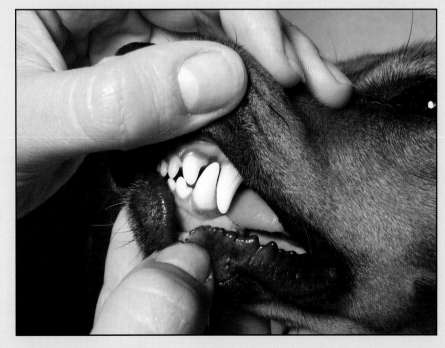

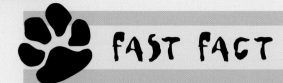

FAST FACT

Don't be surprised if your Dachshund tries to eat the toothpaste as you're brushing his teeth. Most doggie toothpastes are beef or chicken flavored, and he'll think the paste is a tasty treat.

You can supplement brushing with chew toys and other products that are specifically designed to remove tartar buildup. These toys can be purchased from pet supply stores and may be available through your veterinarian's office.

When you take your Dachshund for his annual checkup, your vet will examine your pet's teeth and check for early signs of periodontal disease. If necessary, your vet can also scale and polish your Dachshund's teeth.

TRAINING

Training will make your Dachshund a better companion. It's a good idea to begin training your puppy as soon as you bring him home. The first 18 months may be especially trying. Dachshunds naturally want to please their owners, but they are also energetic and stubborn. These tendencies tend to clash at training time. However, with patience and the right methods, any Dachshund can be

housebroken and taught to follow household rules and obey basic commands like "sit," "stay," "down," and "come." Mastering these commands will provide the foundation for more advanced training.

Some novice dog owners may decide to take their dogs to a professional trainer or obedience school. A professional dog trainer can teach your Dachshund how to obey, and should also show you how to continue his training at home. The drawback to using a professional trainer is the cost. Trainers charge substantial fees for their services. If you can't afford this expense, you may want to consider an obedience school instead. Obedience schools cost less and accomplish many of the same tasks. Dogs that are enrolled in obedience school attend class with their owners. An instructor leads the class and teaches owners how to issue—and get a dog to obey—basic commands.

With patience and a willingness to work hard and be consistent, even an inexperienced dog owner can mold a puppy into a well-behaved dog. The key is consistency. If you're consistent in teaching your Dachshund the rules, he'll be eager to please and will learn quickly. If, on the other hand, you constantly change commands or let him get away with a certain

Puppies use their mouths to explore the world around them. You may think your dog's nips are cute when he's a puppy, but you'll be better off curbing this behavior from the beginning.

behavior one time but not the next, your puppy will become confused and won't respond to your training methods.

No matter how you decide to train your Dachshund, it is important to be kind, patient, and gentle. You should never hit a dog or dole out physical punishment when your puppy misbehaves. The only thing a dog will learn from this is that you are mean. The best way to get a Dachshund to stop doing something is to direct him to the correct behavior and praise him when he acts appropriately. Always remember that training is an ongoing process. If you are kind and consistent, your puppy will eventually pick up on everything you are trying to teach him.

To start, you'll need to teach your puppy that certain behaviors are not acceptable. Biting is a behavior that must be addressed early. It's normal for a puppy to bite and chew when playing with his littermates, and it's normal for him to try this with humans as well. The problem is that human skin isn't quite as tough as puppy skin. To get your puppy to stop biting, you should say "Ouch" or make a noise that will startle him

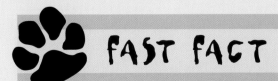

FAST FACT

Treats should always be fed in moderation. Too many treats will make a Dachshund obese and unhealthy.

every time he bites. Then, ignore the puppy for a moment. When you start playing with him again, praise him as long as he's not biting. If he bites, startle him and ignore him again. Eventually, he will get the message that biting is not appropriate.

You'll also want your Dachshund to learn that it's not all right to jump up on people in greeting. Although Dachshunds are small, they can hurt themselves or a guest this way. Curb this behavior early by placing the puppy's front feet on the ground and making him stand still every time a guest enters. Give him praise when he does this correctly. This will demonstrate the behavior you expect.

HOUSEBREAKING

Housebreaking a Dachshund can be a challenge. Like other dogs, Dachshunds don't understand why they aren't allowed to relieve themselves inside the house. It will be up to you to teach your puppy that this is an unacceptable behavior.

It often takes a minimum of six months for a puppy to gain control of his bladder and get into a proper

If you are consistent, your Dachshund puppy will soon learn that the appropriate place to "do his business" is outside the house.

routine. Until then, there will be plenty of accidents. But that's okay. Accidents are an inevitable part of raising and housebreaking a puppy.

Accidents are not a puppy's fault. They are part of the learning process. They may also be unavoidable. Dachshund puppies have very small bladders. Holding urine in for more than a couple of hours is physically impossible for some puppies. Over time, they will gain more control. Until then, however, they will feel the need to eliminate every hour or two. They will also want to go when they first wake up, after they eat, and following playtime.

It is important to let your puppy outside during these times. If you are not able to let your puppy out as needed, you should consider hiring a pet sitter or dog walker to do it for you. Dachshunds that are permitted to eliminate on the carpet and floor when they're home alone during part of the day do not understand why they cannot continue this behavior whenever it pleases them.

Dachshunds can be trained either to relieve themselves outside, or to relieve themselves inside the house on paper. Outside is the preferred spot for most owners. Regardless of the spot you choose, you need to stick with it. Training a puppy to go outside and then switching to paper

FAST FACT

Puppies need to use the potty frequently. As a rule of thumb, a puppy can hold it one hour for every month of his age. A two-month-old puppy can hold it for up to two hours, a three-month-old puppy for three hours, and so on. Always keep in mind, however, that eating, sleeping, and exercising also influence your puppy's need to eliminate.

when it is convenient for you can be confusing for the puppy and may lead to lengthy setbacks.

Technique is just as important as consistency. Many dog experts recommend using a crate to confine and housebreak a puppy. This may seem cruel but actually is not. Crates are easy for puppies to keep clean. They are small and den-like. Since dogs do not like to relieve themselves where they sleep, they will try to avoid going in their den for as long as possible.

If you don't want to crate your Dachshund, you can confine him to a small area of the house while you are away. A laundry room, kitchen, or another room that does not have carpet will work well for this purpose.

When your puppy does have an accident, keep your cool. Getting angry or upset won't accomplish

FAST FACT

A Dachshund puppy that has regular feeding times is easier to housebreak than a Dachshund that eats at different times throughout the day.

anything and in most cases will just make the situation worse. You should also avoid physical punishment. Spanking a dog—or worse, rubbing his nose in his own urine—will not teach him to go outside. It will, however, teach him that you are a cruel person who should not be trusted.

If you see your puppy start to eliminate indoors, call his name, clap your hands, or say something to get his attention. Then tell him, "Outside! Potty outside!" and quickly escort him to the approved area. At the potty place, calmly encourage

FAST FACT

When your puppy has an accident, it is essential that you clean up the mess as thoroughly as you can. Dogs like to eliminate in the same place again and again. Any scent that is left behind will encourage more accidents and bad behavior.

him to eliminate, and praise him when he does. Don't punish him for eliminating in an improper place.

If you don't catch your pup in time and you discover a potty accident after the fact, get a paper towel and take the pup back to the accident spot. Don't scold or shame him, just calmly blot up the pee or pick up the poop in the paper towel, then gently escort your pup to the elimination area. Smear the pee or drop the poop there, then step back and calmly praise your pup, "Good potty outside," as you would if he had gone there to begin with. Your puppy will learn that there's a "good place" to do potty business, and with your help and patience he will learn to use that area.

TEACHING BASIC COMMANDS

There are several basic commands you should teach your puppy before he's six months old: sit, down, stay, and come. It's almost never too early to begin. In fact, the sooner you start, the better. Just remember to keep the training sessions short and fun. Puppies have limited attention spans, and will become bored and willful if training goes on too long.

SIT: Teaching your puppy to sit is one of the easiest ways to control his behavior. To start, get the puppy's attention with a small treat held in your hand. Hold the treat above his nose and tell him to sit. Make sure he has to reach up to get it, but does not have to jump. He should fall naturally into the sitting position. If not, you can very gently push down on his haunches (his rear end, right below the spine and between the hip joints). When he sits down, praise him enthusiastically and give him a piece of the treat. Repeat this exercise for two minutes straight, three to four times a day.

DOWN: Once your dog has mastered the sit command, you can build on this knowledge to teach him to lie down on command. Once again, you'll use a treat to encourage the appropriate response. Start by getting your Dachshund into a sitting position. Hold the treat in front of him at nose level, then give the command, "Down." It may help to use his name first, to make sure you have his attention. At the same time, move the treat down and away from his face.

Your Dachshund should lean forward and follow the treat down. Once his belly touches the ground, reward him with praise and the treat. Practice this exercise for two minutes, three or four times a day.

STAY/COME: The stay and come commands go hand in hand, which means you can teach your puppy to stay and come simultaneously. Begin by getting your Dachshund to sit. Then, holding your hand up like a stop sign, give the command, "Stay." Be sure to say it in a firm voice. If your puppy remains in the sitting position, give him lots of praise. Repeat the exercise, only this time, back away slowly as you issue the stay command. When you get a step or two away from your pup, tell him to come. You can use a treat for extra encouragement. Repeat both the stay and come portion of the exercise for at least two minutes straight, three to four times a day, gradually increasing the distance between you and your pup.

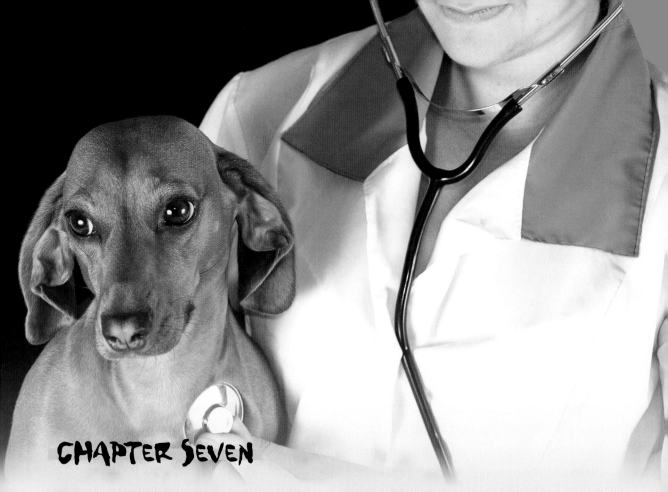

CHAPTER SEVEN

Health Issues Your Dachshund May Face

Dachshunds are a relatively healthy breed, but they can suffer from hereditary conditions and other common medical issues. Taking proper care of your dog by providing good nutrition, regular exercise, and proper preventative health care can help ensure that he has a healthy, happy life. Fortunately, you won't be alone. There are many good veterinarians who can help you develop a feeding

Adult Dachshunds should be examined by a veterinarian at least once a year.

schedule, an exercise regimen, and a health-care plan.

Your pet will need to visit the vet regularly for vaccinations. He will also need periodic wellness exams. Every Dachshund should be given an initial checkup while still a puppy. A good breeder will make sure that a veterinarian examines her puppies soon after they are born; however, you should still plan to take your Dachshund pup for a wellness check within 48 hours after bringing him home. Dachshunds also need exams at six months and one year old. After age one, Dachshunds should be taken for a wellness exam at least once each year until they reach senior status, at about nine years old. After that point, a checkup every six months is recommended.

Wellness exams are the best way to evaluate your pet's general health. These exams can also make you and your vet aware of potential health problems before they become serious conditions or illnesses. When conducting a wellness exam, the vet will check your Dachshund for any unusual lumps and bumps, and will examine his eyes, ears, teeth, and feet. Some vets also perform labs tests, such as a urinalysis, heartworm check, or blood panel, to verify the health of internal organs and systems.

CHOOSING A VETERINARIAN

Selecting a veterinarian is an important decision, and you'll want to take care to find the right one. The vet you choose will be your partner in making essential decisions about your Dachshund's health and lifestyle. The best vets are experienced, competent, patient, and kind.

Look for a veterinarian whose clinic is affiliated with the American Animal Hospital Association or a similar organization that inspects and accredits veterinary facilities.

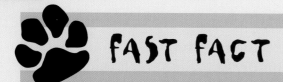

FAST FACT

Each year, Americans spend an estimated $10 billion on health care for their pets.

They are willing to take time to answer questions as they arise. Good vets also have clean facilities with up-to-date equipment.

If you're a first-time pet owner, consider asking family members, friends, or neighbors who have a pet whether they can recommend their veterinarian. You can also request a recommendation from the American Animal Hospital Association (AAHA.) The AAHA is the only companion animal veterinarian association in the United States. This organization has established high standards of quality for veterinarians and facilities. Vets who are members of the AAHA meet these standards, and their

FAST FACT

When you take your puppy to the vet for the first time, you should take your puppy's vaccination records, pedigree papers, and any other documents the breeder gave you.

facilities are regularly inspected by the organization.

Recommendations can lead you to a good vet, but there are other important factors to consider as well, such as the distance from your home to the vet's office. When you have a real emergency, precious minutes could mean the difference between life and death. In other words, having to drive an hour to get to the vet's office may not be the best thing for your pet.

You'll also need to find someone you can truly count on in an emergency. If your Dachshund ingests something poisonous or gets injured on a Sunday afternoon, it's reassuring to know that help is just a phone call away. Most vets have a specific policy with regard to after-hour emergencies. Some handle these cases themselves; others use a calling service or refer patients to a local animal hospital. You should ask prospective veterinarians to explain their emergency policies in detail so you can make an informed decision.

Before making a final decision, interview prospective vets and tour their facilities. A tour will give you a chance to see how clean a clinic is, and to meet the veterinarian and her staff. Trust your judgment. If the staff seems unkind or if the facility looks dirty and unkempt, you will be much better off finding another vet.

WHAT TO EXPECT FROM YOUR FIRST VET VISIT

You should take your new Dachshund to the vet within 48 hours of picking him up. This first visit will consist of a physical exam and a socialization checkup. Physical exams usually begin with a weigh-in and a temperature check. The vet will let you know if your Dachshund is underweight or overweight and, if so, what should be done about it.

The vet will then examine the puppy to make sure he is healthy, checking the puppy's ears, eyes, nose, mouth, and genitals before moving on to the skin and coat. Most vets will also listen to the puppy's heartbeat and check for parasites, hernias, and other health problems.

The vet should keep you updated throughout the exam, but you should not hesitate to ask any questions you might have. As a pet owner, it is your responsibility to know what is happening with your pet's health. You may also want to tell the veterinarian anything unusual that you've noticed about the puppy's body or habits, as this information may be helpful during the initial exam.

When the physical exam is complete, your vet will conduct a social-ization checkup to make sure your puppy is developing properly. This will usually consist of a few simple tests. Afterward, the vet will be able to tell you if your puppy is submissive, dominant, independent, or neutral. All of this information will be helpful when it comes time to housebreak and train your Dachshund.

Many vets will also want to conduct lab tests to check for parasites. This will require a fecal sample from your dog. You should take a fresh sample with you when you go. The sample can be placed in a plastic baggie or container and given to the veterinarian staff when you arrive.

VACCINATIONS

There are many diseases that can have a serious, or potentially fatal, effect on your Dachshund. Inoculations will help protect your Dachshund from the worst of these

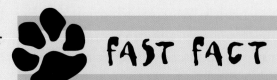

FAST FACT

Dogs can have adverse reactions to certain vaccinations. After receiving a shot, your dog may seem lethargic, have a lack of appetite, or suffer from fever, muscle aches, facial swelling, or vomiting. If your Dachshund exhibits any of these symptoms, call the vet immediately.

Vaccine protocols change periodically as more research is done on canine immunity. Your veterinarian will propose a vaccination schedule that will be appropriate for your dog.

illnesses. Vaccinations will continue throughout the dog's life. Some vaccinations are optional, but most are required to keep your Dachshund in good health. Your veterinarian will be able to tell you which vaccinations your pet needs based on your location and lifestyle. Diseases and viruses your Dachshund should be protected from include:

CANINE PARVOVIRUS: Canine parvovirus, also known as parvo, is a highly contagious disease. There are two forms of this disease: cardiac and intestinal. Both can be transmitted from dog to dog through fecal matter. The virus can live for up to one year in the soil, and up to 10 days on feet, hair, and other objects. Canine parvovirus is treatable if caught early, though even then the prognosis isn't great: half the dogs treated for parvovirus will die. Dogs that are not treated will die 90 percent of the time. Most deaths occur 24 to 72 hours after initial symptoms appear. Those symptoms include severe vomiting, bloody diarrhea, and a high fever. All puppies are extremely susceptible to parvovirus, but small breeds such as Dachshunds are more vulnerable than others. It is important to have your puppy vaccinated at the earliest opportunity. You should also keep your Dachshund away from other dogs and avoid walks in the park until all parvovirus inoculations are complete.

CORONAVIRUS: Canine coronavirus is a highly contagious virus that affects the intestinal tract of dogs. It can be transmitted through contact with fecal matter. The disease is not always life threatening, but it can cause a variety of health problems, including dehydration and respiratory issues. Puppies that have contracted coronavirus are more susceptible to parvovirus infection. Complications can arise if an animal is infected with both at the same time. With the right medication, dogs can recover quickly. Most, however, will remain carriers of the disease for up to six months after recovery. Initial symptoms of canine coronavirus include depression, fever, loss of appetite, vomiting, and diarrhea. Some vets will combine the coronavirus vaccine with vaccines for other diseases. Other vets consider the vaccine unnecessary. Your vet will be able to help you determine whether or not your

Dachshund puppy needs to be inoculated against coronavirus.

DISTEMPER: Distemper is a highly contagious disease related to measles. This dangerous virus can be transmitted through the air and through contact with urine, nasal secretions, and fecal matter. Virtually incurable, it is frequently fatal to small dogs like Dachshunds. Infected dogs that do recover are almost always left paralyzed or partially paralyzed, and they often suffer irreparable damage to their nervous system and respiratory system. Dogs that contract distemper will begin to exhibit symptoms of the disease within two weeks of being infected. Initial symptoms include vomiting, diarrhea, runny nose, weeping eyes, coughing, and a poor appetite. Puppies from three to six months old are especially vulnerable to distemper and must be vaccinated at the earliest opportunity.

HEPATITIS: Also known as canine adenovirus (CAV), infectious canine hepatitis is a contagious infection of the liver. Infected dogs, wolves, coyotes, bears, and other wildlife transmit the disease through feces, urine, blood, saliva, or eye and nasal discharge. The virus attacks the liver and the kidneys. It may cause bleeding disorders and, in extreme cases, death. Generally, healthy Dachshunds can recover after a brief illness, although many will suffer permanent kidney and liver damage. Initial symptoms of canine hepatitis are fever, depression, coughing, poor appetite, vomiting, a tender abdomen, and diarrhea. Dachshund puppies are especially susceptible to this infection and should be vaccinated as soon as possible.

KENNEL COUGH: Also known as tracheobronchitis, kennel cough is a

VACCINATION SCHEDULE

According to the American Kennel Club, Dachshund puppies should receive their first inoculations at five to six weeks of age. However, veterinarians often have different vaccination protocols. Some prefer to wait until a puppy is at least eight weeks old before administering the first vaccinations. In any case, your Dachshund should receive all inoculations required for the first year (except a rabies shot) by the time he is 16 weeks old.

Here is a typical Dachshund vaccination schedule:

6 to 8 Weeks: First distemper, hepatitis, leptospirosis, parainfluenza, parvovirus shot. This is typically given in one combined injection known as the DHLPP shot or simply as the distemper shot.

10 to 12 Weeks: Second DHLPP shot.

14 to 16 Weeks: Third and final DHLPP shot.

3 to 6 Months: Rabies shot. Although this shot may be given to puppies as young as 12 weeks, some states will not recognize rabies vaccinations administered to puppies under 16 weeks. Your veterinarian should be able to tell you more about the laws in your state.

Adult: Booster shots. After receiving initial inoculations, adult dogs need regular booster shots to protect against rabies, distemper, hepatitis, leptospirosis, parainfluenza, and parvovirus.

Depending on your lifestyle and location, your Dachshund may need additional vaccines for coronavirus, kennel cough, and Lyme disease. Coronavirus and kennel cough vaccines can be administered after a puppy is five weeks old. Lyme disease vaccinations can be started after 12 weeks of age and are usually given in two doses three weeks apart. All three vaccines require annual booster shots.

highly contagious illness that affects the respiratory system of canines. The illness can be transmitted through the air, through contact with contaminated surfaces, or through direct contact. Kennel cough is manageable, but it can progress to pneumonia if left untreated. Pneumonia can be fatal in puppies and even in older dogs. Symptoms of kennel cough typically begin three to five days after a dog has been infected. Initial symptoms include coughing, retching, sneezing, and vomiting. Some dogs will also become sensitive to light. A vaccine is recommended for Dachshunds that spend time at the pet groomer, obedience school, kennel, and other places that contain multiple dogs.

LEPTOSPIROSIS: Leptospirosis is a potentially fatal bacterial disease that is becoming more common worldwide. It damages the liver and kidneys of humans, cats, dogs, and other animals. Leptospirosis is most often carried in the urine of rats. Infected animals transmit the disease through blood or urine, which can contaminate soil and water. Recovered animals can also be carriers, and may continue to transmit the disease for months or even years. Leptospirosis can lead to renal failure and death. The disease

is treatable with penicillin if caught early enough. Dogs that do recover may suffer irreparable damage to their liver and kidneys. The earliest symptoms of leptospirosis include fever, vomiting, diarrhea, poor appetite, stiffness, jaundice, internal bleeding, muscle pain, blood in the urine, depression, and lethargy. Some Dachshund puppies with leptospirosis will not exhibit any symptoms, which can make this disease difficult to catch in the early stages. For this reason, it is important to vaccinate your puppy as soon as possible.

LYME DISEASE: Lyme disease is an infectious bacterial illness that affects animals and humans. It is transmitted through the bite of an

Deer ticks are only about the size of a pin head, making them smaller than the more common wood tick. But these tiny parasites carry Lyme disease, which can cause serious health problems for your Dachshund.

infected tick. Lyme disease can cause lameness, kidney problems, and other serious health issues. In rare cases, it can be fatal. Symptoms include lethargy, fever, muscle pain, vertigo, and neurological problems. The vaccine for Lyme disease can interfere with a dog's immune system. If you don't live in a high-risk area, your veterinarian may advise against this inoculation.

PARAINFLUENZA: Parainfluenza is a highly contagious viral infection that causes respiratory problems. If left untreated, it can lead to pneumonia and death. Infected animals usually transmit the virus through nasal secretions. Initial symptoms of parainfluenza include fever, loss of appetite, and a dry, hacking cough. The vaccine for this virus should be administered to your Dachshund puppy as soon as possible.

RABIES: Rabies is a viral disease that attacks the brain. Infected wildlife can transmit this disease to dogs through a bite and other forms of contact. Humans can also be infected with rabies. This disease is almost always fatal to dogs, and if untreated it is also fatal to humans. Animals that have contracted rabies will die within 10 days of being infected.

Initial symptoms include fever, restlessness, aggressiveness, foaming at the mouth, lethargy, mania, and paralysis. Infected animals may also be sensitive to light. All states require dogs to be vaccinated against rabies. Your vet will be able to tell you how soon your Dachshund puppy can receive an inoculation for this deadly disease.

PARASITE CONTROL

Internal and external parasites, such as fleas, ticks, and worms, can cause serious medical problems for your Dachshund and for your family. Children are particularly susceptible to some of the internal parasites that dogs can carry. To keep everyone in good health, you must do your best to prevent the following internal and external parasites:

FLEAS: Fleas are vicious little parasites. They clamp on to your Dachshund's hair and can lay up to 100 eggs on a daily basis. The eggs hatch quickly, which means it won't

FAST FACT

Fleas need to feed on blood to reproduce. However, these pests can live for months without feeding.

take long for your pet and your home to become completely infested. Some dogs are allergic to flea saliva and suffer terrible reactions when bitten. Severe flea problems can also lead to hair loss, anemia, and various illnesses. Flea infestations are a nightmare to eliminate. Fortunately, products such as flea collars can prevent infestations.

MITES: Mites are external parasites. There are six types of mites that attack dogs. All cause some form of mange. Certain types of mange, such as sarcoptic mange (scabies), are extremely contagious and can be passed to other animals as well as to humans. In nearly every case, your Dachshund will itch like crazy. Hair loss, dandruff, and dry skin may also occur. The most severe mite infestations can cause serious medical problems. If caught early on, however, every form of mange is treatable by a veterinarian.

ELIMINATING A FLEA INFESTATION

Once your Dachshund picks up fleas, you'll have to wage an all-out war to rid yourself of these irritating parasites. Each adult flea can lay 20 to 30 batches of up to 100 eggs, and most of these eggs will fall off your dog inside your house. There, within several days to several months, they will hatch. Fleas aren't choosy—if you look tasty, they may hop on you, as well as on your Dachshund. If you don't start a counterattack quickly, you'll soon have a serious flea infestation on your hands.

The first step is to bathe your dog with a veterinarian-recommended flea shampoo. Follow the directions carefully so that it will be effective. Next, while your pet is drying in a room with the door closed, thoroughly vacuum the rest of the house. Pay special attention to carpets and baseboards, where fleas like to hide. Then vacuum the room the dog was in. Unfortunately, you'll have to repeat this whole-house vacuuming routine every day for several weeks. Each time, be sure to empty the vacuum outside and put the contents in a sealed garbage bag.

Regular flea baths and daily vacuuming will enable you to get a flea problem under control. If the problem inside your house seems especially stubborn, you can purchase some insect growth regulator from a pet supply store. Apply it around the house according to the directions on the package.

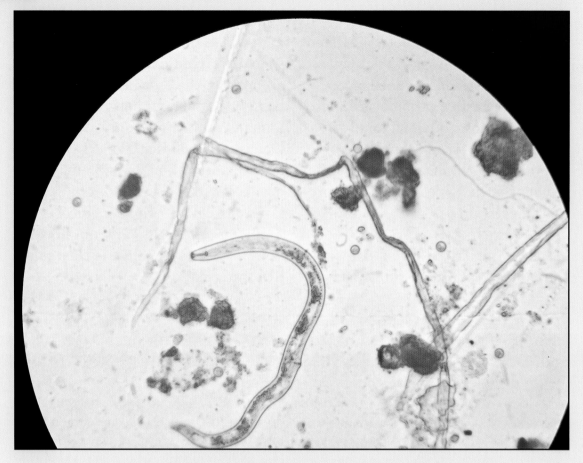

Parasitic worms, like the roundworms shown in this magnified view of infected soil, can cause a variety of health problems in Dachshunds.

TICKS: Ticks are often found in hot and humid areas. These external parasites are not as common as fleas, but they can wreak just as much havoc. Ticks can transmit to dogs Lyme disease, spotted fever, and many other diseases. These parasites are generally controlled and prevented the same way as fleas. Your Dachshund can also be vaccinated for Lyme disease for extra protection. If you see a tick on your dog, remove it immediately. Using tweezers, grasp the tick close to its head and pull it off, then use alcohol to disinfect the site. The longer a tick remains embedded in your dog's skin, the greater the chance it will transmit a tick-borne disease to your dog.

HEARTWORMS: Heartworms are very common in many areas of the country and can be transmitted to your dog by infected mosquitoes. These internal parasites set up shop in your dog's heart and lungs. If your pet is affected by heartworms, he may appear weak, lose weight, or have a serious cough. Left untreated, heartworms can cause death. There are ways to prevent heartworms, but the preventive medicines can compromise a Dachshund's immune system. Talk to your vet to determine whether or not you should give your pet preventive medication.

HOOKWORMS: Hookworms are internal parasites commonly transmitted from mother to puppy, but they can also be contracted if a dog comes into contact with soil or feces that has been infested with roundworm eggs. Hookworms can cause serious anemia and diarrhea and are dangerous to both dogs and humans. Symptoms of a hookworm infestation include dark stool, weight loss, skin problems, and physical weakness. Your veterinarian can easily treat hookworms and may be able to provide you with a preventive medication.

ROUNDWORMS: Like hookworms, roundworms are internal parasites that can be transferred from mother to puppy or through exposure to contaminated soil or feces. Roundworms can be fatal to puppies and may cause serious problems in

adult dogs. They can infect people too. No preventive medicines are 100 percent effective against roundworms, so you should get your Dachshund tested on an annual basis. If you notice any spaghetti-like worms in your pet's feces, contact your vet right away.

TAPEWORMS: Various species of tapeworm can come from uncooked meat and fish, but the usual cause of this internal parasite is fleas. Fleas carry tapeworm and can transmit it to your dog. The tapeworm cycle begins as soon as your dog eats a flea. Tapeworms aren't usually life threatening to dogs; however, they can cause liver disease and other medical problems. If your Dachshund begins losing weight, or if you see evidence of tapeworm in his stool, you should contact your vet immediately for the appropriate worm medication. You should also treat both your dog and home for fleas to prevent the return of tapeworms.

WHIPWORMS: Whipworms are considered the worst of all internal parasites because they are so hard to detect and so difficult to treat. The only way for a vet to determine that your dog is infested with whipworms is by examining the dog's fecal matter, a method that is not always foolproof. Whipworms are acquired from contaminated soil or feces and can cause colic, stomach pain, diarrhea, and weight loss. Treatment is tricky, but available.

Parasites are much easier to prevent than they are to eradicate. Your vet will be able to offer you information on the various types of preventive medicine available. The vet can also test your Dachshund annually to make sure there are no unseen problems.

DACHSHUND-SPECIFIC HEALTH PROBLEMS

There are several hereditary health problems that are frequently seen in Dachshunds. Some of these medical issues affect puppies, while others more commonly plague adult dogs. Many of the following conditions can be treated if caught early enough:

ACANTHOSIS NIGRICANS: Although the term *Acanthosis Nigricans* is sometimes used to describe skin reactions and problems in other breeds, it is actually a very rare disease that exclusively affects Dachshunds. The disease shows itself initially through a darkening of the skin in the armpit areas. The skin will become very dark and tough, and lesions develop that lead to hair loss.

Dogs that are severely affected may have itchy lesions in other areas, such as the chest, belly, groin, and legs. They may also experience bacterial and yeast overgrowth on the skin.

Scientists do not understand what causes Acanthosis Nigricans, and it cannot be cured. However, the disease can be managed to a certain extent through the use of special shampoos, lotions, and other therapies. Dachshunds that suffer from this genetic condition will usually begin to exhibit symptoms before they are a year old.

CUSHING'S SYNDROME: Also known as hyperadrenocorticism, Cushing's syndrome is an endocrine disorder frequently seen in Dachshunds, terriers, poodles, and certain other breeds. The syndrome is most common in dogs that are at least six years old. Cushing's syndrome is usually caused by an abnormality in the pituitary gland. The abnormality causes the adrenal glands to secrete

FAST FACT

Obesity can increase the severity of many of the diseases seen in Dachshunds. For this reason alone, it is important to keep your dog slim and trim.

an excess of cortisol, a hormone usually released in response to stress or anxiety. Cortisol affects many of the body's functions, including metabolism, immune response, and inflammatory response.

The initial symptoms of Cushing's syndrome include increased drinking, appetite, and urination. As the condition progresses, Dachshunds may also suffer from hair loss, thinning skin, wasting muscles, and skin infections. Diagnosis is not always simple, as a tumor can cause similar symptoms. If the veterinarian determines that your Dachshund has Cushing's syndrome, it can be treated with medicine. A tumor must be surgically removed.

ELBOW DYSPLASIA: Elbow dysplasia is a condition commonly seen in larger breeds, but it has also been known to affect Dachshunds. It often occurs when the cartilage in the elbow joint does not develop properly. Initial symptoms of elbow dysplasia include stiffness, limited movement, abnormal posture or gait, pain, reluctance to walk or exercise, and swelling of the joint. If untreated, this condition can also lead to lameness in one or both front legs, as well as degenerative arthritis.

Symptoms of elbow dysplasia usually appear in Dachshunds between six and twelve months of age. While this is a hereditary condition, dysplasia can also be caused by trauma to the elbow at any age. Obesity can make the problem worse. Treatments for elbow dysplasia include pain medication, anti-inflammatory drugs, exercise therapy, and surgery.

EPILEPSY: Dachshunds are one of several breeds affected by epilepsy. This disorder can be caused by brain tumors, birth injuries, head injuries, and exposure to poisonous substances like lead, mercury, or certain insecticides. Dogs with epilepsy experience occasional seizures lasting up to ten minutes. Seizures typically begin with sudden stiffness in limbs, followed by collapse, shaking, and unconsciousness. Although seizures may occur without warning, some owners may notice warning signs in their dog's behavior a few hours or even days before an epileptic attack occurs. These differences can include pacing, whining,

FAST FACT

Dachshunds with genetic diseases should never be bred. There is always a chance that the disease will be passed on to puppies.

growling, hiding, an increased need for closeness, unfounded aggression, and other mood changes. With proper treatment—which may involve anything from medication to acupuncture—epileptic dogs can live a long, normal life.

HIP DYSPLASIA: Some dog breeds, including Dachshunds, have a genetic tendency toward hip dysplasia. This condition is the result of an abnormality in the development of the hip joint. Dachshunds that suffer from hip dysplasia are born with normal hips but develop problems as they grow. Initial symptoms include difficulty walking or jumping. As the condition progresses, dogs will lose strength and may need help getting up to their feet.

Hip dysplasia is a genetic problem, but environmental factors can make this condition worse. Common treatments include medication, weight management, and corrective or hip-replacement surgery. Generally, the treatment method will depend on the dog's age as well as the extent of the dysplasia.

INTERVERTEBRAL DISC DISEASE: Intervertebral disc disease, also known as IVDD or slipped disc disease, is an inherited spine condition that affects about 20 percent of all Dachshunds. This debilitating disease occurs when a disk bulges, ruptures, or slips in the middle of the back. The first signs of IVDD are weakness and lack of coordination. Paralysis can also occur in the most severe cases. Dogs that suffer from IVDD almost always need surgery to repair the disc. If the dog still exhibits some sensation in his hind legs prior to surgery, it is highly likely that he will regain his ability to walk after successful surgery and rehabilitative care.

MEDIAL PATELLAR LUXATION: Medial patellar luxation (MPL) is a congenital anomaly commonly seen in small breeds like Dachshunds. This condition occurs when the kneecap, or patella, becomes dislocated and rides on the inside of its normal groove. MPL causes a degree of lameness. Initial symptoms can include pain and a hitch in the gait. You may also see your dog extend his leg in an attempt to get the knee to pop back into place. The problem may go unnoticed for some time but usually gets progressively worse. The most common treatment is surgery. When a dog is treated early, the chances of a full recovery are high.

NARCOLEPSY: Narcolepsy is an inherited sleep disorder that typically affects Dachshunds and a few other breeds. This condition causes dogs to lose control of their limbs and collapse in complete paralysis. To a bystander, it appears that the dog simply stopped in his tracks and fell asleep. Narcoleptic attacks can last anywhere from a few seconds to a few minutes. Some dogs will slip from paralysis into sleep, but most will stand up and go about their business as though nothing happened. Dogs with narcolepsy will exhibit signs of the condition by the time they are six months old. Attacks come without warning: they may occur once a year or multiple times each day. Most dogs will experience fewer attacks as they age.

Narcolepsy is not a debilitating disease, and does not lead to other illnesses or conditions. The main health risk posed to narcoleptic Dachshunds is the potential for injury if the dog is in the wrong place at the wrong time (on a stairway, for instance) when an attack occurs. To reduce the number of attacks, a veterinarian may prescribe a stimulant or antidepressant.

PROGRESSIVE RETINAL ATROPHY: Progressive Retinal Atrophy (PRA) is one of the most common eye problems seen in the Dachshund breed. Symptoms of this hereditary eye condition are usually evident by the time the dog is two years old. However, most dogs will rely on their senses of smell and hearing to compensate for their declining vision. The condition gets progressively worse as a dog ages, and often results in blindness. There is no treatment for Progressive Retinal Atrophy.

VON WILLEBRAND'S DISEASE: Von Willebrand's disease is an inherited disorder that prevents blood from clotting properly. Affected dogs can bleed to death after an injury or during a routine surgery. Certain breeds, such as Dachshunds, have a higher incidence of Von Willebrand's disease. Symptoms include excessive bleeding, regular nosebleeds, bleeding of the gums, bloody stools, or blood in the urine. Dogs who have bleeding in their joints may also exhibit symptoms of arthritis. There is no known cure for Von Willebrand's disease. Dogs that are bleeding uncontrollably after surgery or an injury may be treated with blood transfused from a healthy dog.

CHAPTER EIGHT

Enjoying and Caring For Your Dachshund

Caring for an adult Dachshund isn't much different from caring for a puppy. As an adult, your pet will still need plenty of love, attention, and guidance. The difference is that you will probably have more time to devote to these things once your dog is housebroken and able to follow basic commands.

You can use this extra time to have fun with your Dachshund. Together, you can explore a wide range of new activities. Activities that older Dachshunds may enjoy include dog shows and trials or hunting. Many Dachshunds also enjoy traveling and will be more than willing to explore the world at your side.

An adult Dachshund will be up for almost any activity that involves spending time with you.

ADVANCED TRAINING

The term *advanced training* usually refers to anything beyond basic obedience training (the commands "sit," "down," "stay," and "come"). The following paragraphs offer simple training methods that can be used to teach your Dachshund several new skills, such as how to walk properly both on and off a leash and how to catch and retrieve a ball or other object.

Remember, training takes time and patience. No single training method is right for every dog, so adjust these methods to suit your Dachshund's ability and personality.

WALKING ON A LEASH PROPERLY:

Dogs must be trained not to tug or pull incessantly against the leash. You'll also want your dog to walk at your side, and to stop walking when you do. Before your Dachshund can become a well-behaved walker, he'll have to master the "sit" command.

Start the training exercise by hooking a nylon leash to your dog's collar. Position the dog on your left side and instruct him to sit. Raise your left foot and begin walking. Issue the command "heel" in a firm tone as soon as your foot leaves the ground. If your dog tries to run ahead or lag behind, issue the "heel" command

Your Dachshund should be trained to walk beside you properly on a leash.

once more. Praise your dog when he walks beside you properly.

Keep your dog on your left side as you walk, even when you turn. When you stop, tell the dog to sit. If necessary, pull up on the leash very gently to coax him into a sitting position. When you begin walking again, command your Dachshund to heel. If you repeat the exercise for a few minutes each day, several times per day, and offer encouragement, praise, and the occasional treat for motivation, your Dachshund should learn how to walk on a leash in no time.

WALKING OFF A LEASH: Training a dog to walk without being leashed is very similar to training a dog to walk on a leash. This trick is best taught after your Dachshund has completely mastered the "heel" command. If he cannot behave when he is on a leash, then he is probably not ready to walk without a leash. Off-leash training should be conducted in a fenced-in yard or enclosed area in case your Dachshund runs away in pursuit of a bird, rabbit, or another distraction.

CATCH AND RETRIEVE: Teaching your Dachshund to catch and retrieve can be fun for both you and your pet. This activity is great exercise for dogs. It also provides an opportunity for you and your Dachshund to bond with one another. To get a dog to catch or retrieve anything, you must first get him interested in the object. For example, if you want to teach him to catch and retrieve a ball, then you should get him to want to touch the ball. As soon as your Dachshund takes the ball (or Frisbee or whatever else you are using), give him lots of praise so that he knows you approve.

The next step is getting him to chase the ball when you throw it. Start with low, short throws that are easy for him to follow. If you want your Dachshund to retrieve the ball and bring it back to you, give him a command like "fetch" or "retrieve" as you throw the object. Once he has the ball, coax him into bringing the ball back by calling his name or giving the "come" command. If necessary, use a treat as extra encouragement.

If you want your Dachshund to catch a ball, throw it gently into the air in his direction while issuing the command "catch." Be sure to use a soft ball so that your Dachshund won't be hurt if he misses and the ball hits him in the face.

PARTICIPATING IN COMPETITIONS

Showing dogs is a sport that combines competition with a love of dog breeds. Dachshunds are just one of the many breeds that owners like to show off. In the United States, Dachshunds are classified as hounds,

FAST FACT

Do not use a choke collar when teaching your Dachshund to walk on leash. This sort of equipment will make your pet scared and nervous. A regular collar and leash should be sufficient when training a dog to walk properly.

a group that also includes the Beagle, the Bloodhound, and the Irish Wolfhound. The American Kennel Club (AKC) recognizes six other dog groups that participate in competitions. These include sporting breeds (Pointers, Retrievers, Setters), working breeds (Boxer, Doberman Pinscher), terrier breeds (Airedale, Cairn Terrier, Scottish Terrier), toy breeds (Chihuahua, Maltese, Pomeranian), non-sporting breeds (Bulldog, Dalmatian, Poodle), and herding breeds (Collie, German Shepherd, Old English Sheepdog).

Dog shows, also known as conformation events, are just one of the many competitions open to AKC-registered purebreds. Other AKC-sanctioned events include obedience, field, and agility trials, tracking tests, and earthdog tests.

CONFORMATION SHOWS:
Conformation shows were originally developed to showcase breeding stock, so only purebreds that adhere closely to the Standard of Perfection for their breed are permitted to compete. There are three basic types of

If you've got a Dachshund that meets the breed standard, plus has a bit of an attitude, he might do well in Conformation events.

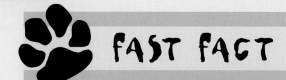

conformation shows: all-breed shows, specialty shows, and group shows. Specialty shows are open to dogs of a specific breed. For example, the Dachshund Club of America holds specialty shows that are just for Dachshunds. Group shows are for dogs of a particular group, such as the hound group. All-breed shows—the type most frequently seen on TV—give dogs in any of the more than 150 AKC-recognized breeds a chance to shine. In such shows, entrants compete first against other dogs of their breed. Next, all the Best of Breed winners within a group are judged to determine Best of Group. After this, the Best of Group winners are evaluated and one dog is named Best in Show.

Dogs who participate in conformation shows are not compared against each other. Instead, they are compared against the Standard of Perfection for their breed. The dog that comes closest to the breed standard usually wins. However, a dog's personality and showmanship can yield extra points.

Showing Dachshunds is not nearly as easy as it looks on television. If you're interested in getting in the ring, you should attend several dog shows and, if possible, enroll your dog in a conformation class. This will help you decide whether you and your dog will enjoy this activity. You must also be ready to commit to doing a great deal of work. A show dog requires more grooming and additional training sessions.

OBEDIENCE TRIALS: Obedience trials focus on a dog's skills rather than his appearance. Competitions can be found for dogs of all skill levels. Special titles or ribbons may be awarded in AKC-sponsored obedience trials. To participate, Dachshunds must be at least six months old. They must also be able to follow basic commands. Required skills can vary depending on the level of competition. Dogs at the novice level are often asked to stand for examination, walk on and off a leash, sit, lie down, come when called, and navigate various obstacles. At the advanced level, dogs may be expected to obey nonverbal commands or distinguish a handler's scent among a pile of items.

FIELD TRIALS: Field trials are designed to test a dog's ability to perform his original purpose in the

DACHSHUND RACING

Dachshund racing, or wiener dog racing as it is also known, is a competitive sporting event for Dachshunds. The first Dachshund racing event was held in Australia during the 1970s. Today, Dachshund racing takes place primarily in the United States.

At most events, several Dachshunds are placed on a track and encouraged to race each other for 25 to 50 yards. Owners usually stand at the end of the track to encourage their Dachshunds with treats or toys.

National, regional, and local wiener dog races are held every single year. Although there are many dogs and Dachshund enthusiasts who enjoy watching and participating in these events, the races are controversial. Organizations like the Dachshund Club of America (DCA) do not approve of Dachshund races. The DCA has taken this stance because of the Dachshund's genetic predisposition to back injuries. Racing can put unnecessary strain on a Dachshund's spinal column and other parts of his body.

The DCA and other animal rights groups also oppose Dachshund racing because they fear breeders and puppy mills will begin to breed "racing" Dachshunds for profit. These new Dachshunds will inevitably add to the already over-populated pet world and may also compromise the Dachshund breed standard that responsible breeders work so hard to follow.

Dachshunds race at a festival in Decatur, Georgia.

HUNTING WITH DACHSHUNDS

Dachshunds are natural hunters. Many dogs of this breed still enjoy the sport today. Dachshunds are best used for hunting small prey, such as badgers, rabbits, or foxes, although some hunters even use these fast little scent-hounds to track larger animals, like deer.

Although hunting comes naturally to most Dachshunds, you'll need to test your dog in the field to see whether he shows any aptitude or interest in the sport. You'll also need to work with your Dachshund on a regular basis so that he learns to follow all of your commands in the field. Your dog should be able to sit, stay, come, walk off a leash, track, and retrieve an object consistently before he'll be ready for hunting. There may be clubs or classes in your local area where you can learn more about hunting with your Dachshund.

AKC-sponsored field trials, tracking tests, and earthdog competitions measure a Dachshund's ability to hunt its quarry over various terrains.

field. In Dachshund field trials, a pair of dogs of the same gender track the scent of a rabbit. The dogs are judged on how efficiently and successfully they follow their quarry, as well as their enthusiasm for hunting.

AGILITY TRIALS: Like obedience trials, agility trials focus on a dog's skills rather than his looks. In agility trials, dogs compete in obstacle courses. Their owners or handlers guide them through the course. Courses usually include jumps, weave poles, pipe tunnels, and dog walks. Dachshunds can compete in agility trials at four different skill levels. To take part in an AKC-

sanctioned agility event, dogs must be at least one year old.

TRACKING TESTS: These competitions test a dog's ability to follow scents over a specific distance. The AKC administers tracking tests at three different levels and holds a national invitational every year. The three tracking titles that can be earned include Tracking Dog (for following a track of 440 to 500 yards that includes several turns), Tracking Dog Excellent (for following a 1,000-yard track with several turns), and Variable Surface Tracking (for following a scent over three different surfaces on an 800-yard track).

Both Standard Dachshunds and Miniature Dachshunds have the speed, balance, and leaping ability to successfully negotiate the obstacles on an agility course.

bred for this purpose. Dogs can compete in these competitions at four different levels: Introduction to Quarry, Junior Earthdog, Senior Earthdog, and Master Earthdog.

CANINE GOOD CITIZEN TEST

In 1989, the American Kennel Club started a program known as the Canine Good Citizen (CGC) Program. Its goal is to promote well-mannered dogs and responsible pet ownership. Dogs that pass the 10-step obedience test are awarded a certificate from the AKC.

The Canine Good Citizen Test is a pass/fail test. To earn a certificate, Dachshunds must prove that they can accept a friendly stranger, sit and stay on command, sit politely for petting, stand for grooming and examination, walk on a leash, walk through a crowd, come when called, react appropriately to other dogs, stay calm when distracted, and behave when left alone with a friendly stranger for at least three minutes. If a dog does not pass the test on the first attempt, he is allowed to try again.

Dogs of any breed or age are eligible to participate in the test, which is typically administered by dog clubs, community organizations, 4-H groups, and veterinary associations. Participating in the CGC Program is

Dachshunds may be small, but they can have a big impact on people's lives as therapy dogs. Therapy dogs visit local hospitals, rehabilitation centers, and nursing homes to provide companionship and to cheer up residents. If your pet knows how to mind his manners and loves to entertain people with his antics, performing the duties of a therapy dog will come naturally to him.

EARTHDOG TESTS: Earthdog competitions test a dog's ability to go into the ground after quarry. These tests were originally geared toward terrier breeds, but are also open to Dachshunds, which were originally

a good way to reward your dog for having good manners. It also provides a good foundation for participation in other events, such as conformation shows and obedience trials.

TRAVELING WITH YOUR DACHSHUND

Dachshunds make great travel companions. They love to discover new things and are almost always willing to take a trip someplace new. If your dog can handle long rides in the car or on an airplane, there is no reason why he can't come along with you on vacation.

Even if you don't plan to take your Dachshund everywhere you go, you should get him accustomed to traveling in the car as soon as possible. If he isn't used to riding in a car, he will become nervous every time you take him to the vet or to be groomed.

To prepare for car trips, allow your pet to relieve himself before placing him in the vehicle. You should also take along towels and something to clean up after him in case he has an accident or needs an emergency bathroom break. If he seems nervous about being in the car, give him a treat and a gentle pat on the head. You can also distract him by talking to him in a soothing and confident voice. The more confident you sound, the better. If you're nervous, your pet will pick up on that emotion.

Never allow your Dachshund to run loose in the car, as this can be very dangerous. The safest way for a dog to travel is inside an appropriately sized plastic crate. If your Dachshund isn't used to being inside a crate, or finds the confinement too stressful, you can purchase a harness specially made to keep him in the seat. A final alternative is to allow him to ride in a passenger's lap.

Flying with your Dachshund will require some additional preparation. Every airline has different policies when it comes to canine passengers. Some airlines will allow you to take a smaller dog like a Miniature Dachshund on the plane. Others make dogs ride in an area that is separate from human passengers. In either case, your Dachshund will need to be tucked away in a pet carrier or plastic crate before boarding an

Never leave your Dachshund in the car when it's warm! On a 73° Fahrenheit (23° Celsius) day, the temperature inside a closed car can reach 120°F (49°C) in 30 minutes. On a 90°F (32°C) day, the temperature can reach 160°F (71°C) in less than 15 minutes. High temperatures will cause heatstroke, which can kill your Dachshund.

airplane. Some airlines have special guidelines about crate size. Before leaving, check with the airline you'll be using so that you don't have any last-minute problems or expenses.

If your Dachshund can handle air travel or car rides, there is no reason why he can't join you on vacation. Many hotels and resorts accommodate pet owners who want to travel with their dogs. These establishments can be found online at Web sites like PetsWelcome.com, PetTravel.com, and LetsGoPets.com. You may have to pay a security deposit or extra fee for your pet, although some hotels will waive the charge if your dog has an AKC Canine Good Citizen certificate.

Before taking your Dachshund anywhere, make sure that he has proper identification and is up-to-date on his vaccinations. You will also want to take everything you'll need to care for him, including a collar, leash, medications, toys, food, treats, and dishes. Also, pack a sharp color photograph of your dog; you'll need it for posters in case your Dachshund is lost or stolen.

WHEN YOUR DACHSHUND STAYS BEHIND

Pet owners who are unable or unwilling to take their Dachshund on vacation will need to make other arrangements prior to a trip.

Dachshunds cannot be left home alone for long periods of time. Fortunately, there are boarding kennels and doggie day care centers that can care for your pet while you are away.

Boarding kennels are usually willing to take dogs for long periods of time. Doggie day care centers, on the other hand, may not be as accommodating. Facilities in your area can be found by searching the Internet or your local phone book. Friends, family members, or your dog's veterinarian may also be able to recommend good places where your dog can stay.

The level of care can vary greatly from kennel to kennel. At the best

facilities, your dog will receive daily walks, regular play times, and grooming in addition to his feedings. Some facilities will have a veterinarian in house or on call in case your pet is injured or experiences some sort of health problem while you are away.

If you prefer that your pet stay at home, you'll need to ask a trusted friend or family member to visit your house several times each day to feed your Dachshund and let him outside. Another option is a professional pet sitter. Most will come directly to your home, and those who don't will open their own home to your dog. If you decide to take this route, be sure to get recommendations and interview candidates. You don't want to

The boarding kennel or doggie day care center that keeps your dog while you are away should be clean, safe, and large enough to accommodate your pet. There should be separate areas for animals that are sick or aggressive.

As your Dachshund ages, the hair on his muzzle may begin to turn gray.

randomly choose someone for this important job.

CARING FOR YOUR SENIOR PET

Although a Dachshund that receives proper care can live 14 years or more, Dachshunds are usually considered seniors when they are around nine years old. When your pet reaches this age, you may begin noticing changes in his physical appearance and temperament. Gray hair may start to appear around his face and paws. His eating, playing, and sleeping habits may also change.

Don't be surprised if your senior Dachshund begins having accidents in the house again. Incontinence is a normal part of aging for most dogs. Don't get angry at your pet when this happens. He probably feels even worse about it than you do. Barking, whining, and destructive behavior may also occur when your senior Dachshund is upset or left home alone.

These changes can be painful to watch, but they don't have to diminish your pet's quality of life. If you are patient, loving, and understanding, you can make the aging process easier on him.

NUTRITION AND EXERCISE

As your pet ages, his dietary needs will change. An older dog sleeps more and exercises less. Your Dachshund still needs to eat food with the proper combination of protein, carbohydrates, and fiber. However, he should be eating food that is low in fat or one that is specially formulated for senior dogs. Senior dogs need food that is easy to chew and digest. Small kibble is usually best, providing your dog has healthy teeth and the ability to chew kibble.

If you notice your dog is having difficulty chewing or digesting his food, speak to your veterinarian. Most vets will be able to recommend alternative diets that will work for your Dachshund.

Your vet will also help you develop an appropriate exercise regimen for your senior Dachshund. Although older dogs are more prone to aches and pains, they still need to maintain a certain activity level. Your veterinarian will be able to recommend an exercise program based on your dog's age and health.

HEALTH PROBLEMS

There are some age-related health issues that cannot be prevented no matter how well you care for your senior Dachshund. Many of these

You may find that your senior Dachshund enjoys being held and petted even more than he did when he was a younger dog. Although senior dogs are not as active as they used to be, they still need plenty of exercise, proper food, and unconditional love.

problems are incurable, but can be successfully treated with medication if they are diagnosed early. Your veterinarian will be able to help with diagnosis and treatment so that your senior pet can be made as comfortable as possible.

COGNITIVE DYSFUNCTION SYNDROME: Known more commonly as "old-dog syndrome," cognitive dysfunction syndrome (CDS) is the progressive deterioration of cognitive abilities. In plain English, this means your Dachshund is slowing down mentally. Common signs of CDS include sleeping more during the day, frequent potty accidents, confusion or forgetfulness, and a decreased desire to socialize. More than half of all senior dogs have some form of CDS. Treatments include medication and therapy.

HEARING AND VISION LOSS: It is not uncommon for older dogs to suffer from progressive hearing or vision loss. Hearing problems are generally caused by deterioration of the ear. Vision loss can result from cataracts or other age-related issues. Treatment may or may not be available for both, depending on the specific problem.

HEART DISEASE: Older Dachshunds, like humans, can suffer from heart disease. Some of the early symptoms include coughing and labored breathing. Your vet can check for cardiac problems when performing a physical. The vet will also be able to advise you about the various treatment options that are available.

ARTHRITIS: Many senior Dachshunds suffer from arthritis, an extremely painful and degenerative joint disease. Symptoms can be hard to spot at first. But as the disease becomes progressively worse, your pet will move with obvious stiffness. He will also have difficulty jumping on furniture or climbing stairs. He may even become aggressive when the pain becomes unbearable. There is no way to cure arthritis. However, your vet will be able to help you develop a treatment plan using a combination of medicine, supplements, and exercise therapy.

SAYING GOODBYE

Saying good-bye to a beloved pet is one of the hardest things you'll ever have to do. By the time you're required to do this, your Dachshund will have become an integral part of your family.

Unfortunately, very few dogs die peacefully in their sleep. A time may come when you're forced to make the decision to end your pet's life.

This usually happens because of a life-threatening illness that is past the point of curing or treatment. If your Dachshund can no longer enjoy the simple pleasures of life, and is suffering extreme pain or discomfort, euthanasia may be the right choice.

Euthanasia is the planned killing of a dog by means of an injection. The initial poke aside, it's absolutely painless for your dog. Of course, it will be very painful for you. Nobody wants to be forced to put a beloved animal companion to sleep. However, if keeping your Dachshund alive will only prolong his suffering, euthanasia may be the kindest thing you can do.

The death of your companion will no doubt be a traumatic experience. Give yourself time to grieve. If you don't want to go it alone, there are many national and local support groups you can turn to. People in these groups had similar experiences and will understand what you're going through.

If you have other pets, don't be surprised if they go through a grieving period as well. Your Dachshund was part of a pack, and his loss will probably affect everyone in the household.

Although it may be tempting to go out and get another dog immediately to fill the void that you feel, that may not be the best thing to do. A new pet will do much better entering a happy household as opposed to one that is filled with grief. After you and the rest of your family have had an opportunity to make peace with your Dachshund's passing, then you may feel ready to get another dog—perhaps even another Dachshund!

Organizations to Contact

**American Animal
Hospital Association**
12575 West Bayaud Ave.
Lakewood, CO 80228
Phone: 303-986-2800
Fax: 800-252-2242
E-mail: info@aahanet.org
Web site: www.aahanet.org

**American Dog Breeders
Association**
P.O. Box 1771
Salt Lake City, UT 84110
Phone: 801-936-7513
E-mail: bstofshw@adba.cc
Web site: www.adbadogs.com

American Humane Association
63 Inverness Dr. East
Englewood, CO 80112
Phone: 303-792-9900
Fax: 303-792-5333
Web site: www.americanhumane.org

American Kennel Club
8051 Arco Corporate Dr., Suite 100
Raleigh, NC 27617
Phone: 919-233-9767
E-mail: info@akc.org
Web site: www.akc.org

Association of Pet Dog Trainers
150 Executive Center Dr., Box 35
Greenville, SC 29615
Phone: 800-738-3647
Fax: 864-331-0767
E-mail: information@apdt.com
Web site: www.apdt.com

The Canadian Kennel Club
89 Skyway Avenue, Suite 100
Etobicoke, Ontario, M9W 6R4
Canada
Phone: 416-675-5511
Fax: 416-675-6506
E-mail: information@ckc.ca
Web site: www.ckc.ca/en

Dachshund Club of America, Inc.
1793 Berme Road
Kerhonkson, NY 12446
E-mail: candachs@aol.com
Web site: www.dachshund-dca.org

Humane Society of the U.S.
2100 L St., NW
Washington, DC 20037
Phone: 202-452-1100
Fax: 301-548-7701
E-mail: info@hsus.org
Web site: www.hsus.org

**The Kennel Club
of the United Kingdom**
1-5 Clarges St.
Picadilly
London W1J 8AB
United Kingdom
Phone: 0870 606 6750
Fax: 020 7518 1058
Web site: www.thekennelclub.org.uk

**National Association of
Professional Pet Sitters (NAPPS)**
17000 Commerce Parkway, Suite C
Mt. Laurel, NJ 08054
Phone: 856-439-0324
Fax: 856-439-0525
E-mail: napps@ahint.com
Web site: www.petsitters.org

**National Miniature Dachshund
Club, Inc.**
1020 Indian Trail
Lawrenceburg, KY 40342
Phone: 937-839-5431
E-mail: petalpshr@bellsouth.net
Web site: www.dachshund-nmdc.org

**North American Versatile Hunting
Dog Association**
PO Box 520
Arlington Heights, IL 60006
Phone: 847-253-6488
Fax: 847-255-5987
E-mail: navoffice@navhda.org
Web site: www.navhda.org

North American Flyball Assn.
1400 West Devon Ave. #512
Chicago, IL 60660
Phone: 800-318-6312
Web site: www.flyball.org

**Orthopedic Foundation
for Animals (OFA)**
2300 East Nifong Boulevard
Columbia, MO 65201
Phone: 573-442-0418
Fax: 573-875-5073
Web site: www.offa.org

Pet Industry Joint Advisory Council
1220 19th Street, NW Suite 400
Washington, DC 20036
Phone: 202-452-1525
Fax: 202-293-4377
Web site: www.pijac.org

Pet Loss Support Hotline
College of Veterinary Medicine
Cornell University
Ithaca, NY 14853-6401
Phone: 607-253-3932
Web site: www.vet.cornell.edu/
public/petloss

Pet Sitters International (PSI)
201 East King Street
King, NC 27021-9161
Phone: 336-983-9222
Fax: 336-983-9222
Web site: www.petsit.com

Therapy Dogs International, Inc.
88 Bartley Road
Flanders, NJ 07836
Phone: 973-252-9800
Fax: 973-252-7171
E-mail: tdi@gti.net
Web site: www.tdi-dog.org

UK National Pet Register
74 North Albert Street, Dept 2
Fleetwood, Lancasterhire
FY7 6BJ
United Kingdom
Web site: www.nationalpet
        register.org

**United States Dog Agility
Association, Inc. (USDAA)**
P.O. Box 850955
Richardson, TX 75085-0955
Phone: 972-487-2200
Fax: 972-272-4404
E-mail: info@usdaa.com
Web site: www.usdaa.com

Veterinary Medical Databases
1717 Philo Rd.
PO Box 3007
Urbana, IL 61803-3007
Phone: 217-693-4800
E-mail: cerf@vmdb.org
Web site: www.vmdb.org

**World Canine Freestyle
Organization (WCFO)**
PO Box 350122
Brooklyn, NY 11235-2525
Phone: 718-332-8336
E-mail: wcfodogs@aol.com
Web site: www.worldcaninefreestyle.org

Further Reading

Adamson, Eve. *Dachshunds for Dummies*. Hoboken, N.J.: Wiley Publishing Inc., 2007.

Dachshund: Smart Owner's Guide from the Editors of Dog Fancy. Freehold, N.J.: Kennel Club Books, 2009.

Everest, Elaine. *Showing Your Dog: A Beginner's Guide*. Begbroke, Oxford, UK: How To Books, Ltd., 2009.

Fernandez, Amy. *Training Your Dachshund*. Hauppauge, N.Y.: Barron's Educational, 2008.

Jones, Amanda. *Dachshunds Short and Long*. New York: Berkley Trade, 2009.

Landau, Elaine. *Dachshunds Are the Best!* Minneapolis: Lerner Publishing Group, 2010.

Rice, Dan. *The Complete Book of Dog Breeding*. Hauppauge, N.Y.: Barron's Educational, 2008.

Sovey, Melissa. *Doxie Moxie: Little Dog, Big Attitude*. Minocqua, Wis.: Willow Creek Press, 2007.

Webster Boneham, Sheila. *Dachshunds*. Neptune, N.J.: TFH Publications, Inc., 2007.

Young, Peter. *Groom Your Dog Like a Professional*. Neptune, N.J.: TFH Publications, Inc., 2009.

Internet Resources

http://www.akc.org/breeds/dachshund/index.cfm

This page contains the American Kennel Club's description of the Dachshund breed standard.

http://www.aspca.org

The Web site of the American Society for the Prevention of Cruelty to Animals provides expert advice on pet care, animal behavior, poison control, and disaster preparedness.

http://www.ckc.ca/en/Portals/0/pdf/breeds/DML.pdf

This Web page contains the Canadian Kennel Club's breed standard for Dachshunds.

http://www.dachshund-dca.org

The Dachshund Club of America offers breed information, club rules, a pedigree database, a breeder directory, and much more through their official Web site.

http://www.dachshund-nmdc.org

The official Web site of the National Miniature Dachshund Club provides a wealth of information about the Miniature Dachshund and links to helpful resources.

Publisher's Note: The Web sites listed on these pages were active at the time of publication. The publisher is not responsible for Web sites that have changed their address or discontinued operation since the date of publication.

http://www.healthypet.com

The pet owner's Web site of the American Animal Hospital Association lists accredited veterinary hospitals in every state and provides up-to-date pet health information.

http://www.hsus.org

The official Web site of the Humane Society of the United States offers valuable information about pet adoption and pet issues.

http://www.thekennelclub.org.uk/item/18

This page contains a description of the breed standard for Dachshunds as established by The Kennel Club of the United Kingdom.

http://www.westminsterkennelclub.org

This website includes breed information, showmanship videos, and details about the Westminster Dog Show.

Index

Numbers in **bold italics** refer to captions.

Contributors

KAREN SCHWEITZER is a professional writer and dog lover from Michigan. Her books include guides on caring for Shih Tzus and Beagles in the OUR BEST FRIENDS series. She has also written several books for young adults, as well as numerous articles that have been published in major magazines, newspapers, and Web sites.

Senior Consulting Editor **GARY KORSGAARD, DVM,** has had a long and distinguished career in veterinary medicine. After graduating from The Ohio State University's College of Veterinary Medicine in 1963, he spent two years as a captain in the Veterinary Corps of the U.S. Army. During that time he attended the Walter Reed Army Institute of Research and became Chief of the Veterinary Division for the Sixth Army Medical Laboratory at the Presidio, San Francisco.

In 1968 Dr. Korsgaard founded the Monte Vista Veterinary Hospital in Concord, California, where he practiced for 32 years as a small animal veterinarian. He is a past president of the Contra Costa Veterinary Association, and was one of the founding members of the Contra Costa Veterinary Emergency Clinic, serving as president and board member of that hospital for nearly 30 years.

Dr. Korsgaard retired in 2000. He enjoys golf, hiking, international travel, and spending time with his wife Susan and their three children and four grandchildren.